Power

The Secrets of 13 Successful family Companies

Robert Jhonson

Preface

For over two decades, I have stood as a silent witness to the intricate tales of family businesses—stories woven with threads of determination, shared history, and the indomitable spirit that defines generations. In these narratives, the peculiarities of family businesses may seem enigmatic to the untrained eye, yet, with each passing year, I've come to realize that their essence lies not in the visible surface but in the very DNA that courses through their veins.

An Intimate Odyssey

This book, "The Power of Family: Secrets of 13 Successful Companies," is not a distant observation but a culmination of an intimate odyssey. It is born from the conversations shared, the challenges faced, and the triumphs celebrated alongside families who dared to dream collectively. The peculiarities, the idiosyncrasies that make each family business unique—they have become the brushstrokes in a larger portrait of resilience.

Exploring the DNA of Success

As we embark on this exploration, we journey beyond the glossy exterior of global giants and the subtle artistry of niche players. We delve into the DNA of thirteen remarkable companies, each with a story to tell—a story that whispers of triumphs etched in perseverance and strategies rooted in the power of family.

Secrets Unveiled, Lessons Learned

Through in-depth case studies and the discerning lens of expert analysis, we unveil the secrets that lie beneath the surface. These are not tales of overnight success or serendipitous fortune; they are sagas of hard work, innovation, and the ability to adapt to the ever-shifting currents of the market. Readers will find within these pages not just stories but invaluable insights into the dynamics of family involvement, the significance of unwavering core values, and the acumen needed to steer through challenges.

A Blueprint for Success

Whether you're a seasoned business owner steering the helm of your enterprise, an entrepreneur forging new paths, or someone simply curious about the alchemy of successful companies, this book serves as more than a collection of narratives. It is a blueprint for success—a compendium of practical lessons drawn from the lived experiences of those who have not only weathered storms but have harnessed the power of family to build empires that endure.

Beyond the Pages

As you turn these pages, let the stories unfold, not as distant tales, but as companions in your own journey. May the revelations within these chapters inspire and guide, and may the secrets of family businesses become not just stories to be read but lessons to be lived.

Welcome to the intimate world of familial success—a world where the power of family is not just a concept but a force that shapes destinies. Through the anecdotes, may you discover that success is not a solitary pursuit; it is a collective endeavor, a tapestry woven with the threads of resilience, innovation, and the unwavering power of family.

Robert Jhonson

Introduction

1.1 Understanding Family Companies

Family companies have a unique dynamic that sets them apart from other types of businesses. These companies are not only driven by profit and growth but also by a strong sense of family values and traditions. Understanding the inner workings of family companies is crucial to comprehending their success and the lessons that can be learned from them.

Family companies are characterized by their ownership and management being closely tied to one or more families. This means that the decision-making process is often influenced by family members who have a personal stake in the company's success. This can lead to a long-term perspective and a commitment to preserving the company's legacy for future generations.

One of the key advantages of family companies is the ability to maintain a strong sense of identity and purpose. Family values, traditions, and a shared vision are often deeply ingrained in the company's culture. This can create a strong sense of loyalty and commitment among employees, as well as a clear direction for the company's growth.

Family companies also tend to have a long-term perspective when it comes to decision-making. Unlike publicly traded companies that may be driven by short-term financial goals, family companies often prioritize sustainable growth and the preservation of their reputation. This long-term focus allows them to weather economic downturns and make strategic decisions that may not yield immediate results but are beneficial in the long run.

Furthermore, family companies often have a strong commitment to their employees and the communities in which they operate. They prioritize creating a positive work environment, fostering employee development, and giving back to the community. This commitment to social responsibility can enhance the company's reputation and build strong relationships with stakeholders.

However, family companies also face unique challenges that can impact their success. One of the main challenges is the potential for conflicts and tensions within the family itself. Balancing personal relationships with professional responsibilities can be complex and requires effective communication and conflict resolution strategies.

Succession planning is another critical aspect for family companies. Ensuring a smooth transition of leadership from one generation to the next is essential for the company's continuity and growth. This involves identifying and preparing the next generation of leaders, as well as establishing clear governance structures and processes.

Despite these challenges, family companies have achieved remarkable success across various sectors. Let's explore some of the most successful family companies and the lessons that can be learned from them:

- IKEA: IKEA's success can be attributed to its innovative business model, focus on

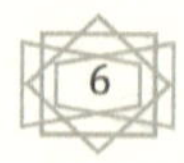

affordability, and commitment to sustainability. The company's flat-pack furniture concept revolutionized the industry, and its strong family values have shaped its culture and customer experience.

- Toyota: Toyota's continuous improvement philosophy, known as "Kaizen," has been instrumental in its success. The company's commitment to quality, efficiency, and innovation has made it a global leader in the automotive industry.

- Ferrero: Ferrero's success lies in its ability to balance tradition and innovation. The company's commitment to quality and product innovation, combined with its strong family values, has made it a household name in the confectionery industry.

- Patagonia: Patagonia's commitment to environmental sustainability and ethical business practices has set it apart in the apparel industry. The company's focus on creating high-quality, durable products while minimizing its environmental impact has resonated with consumers and built a loyal customer base.

- Volkswagen: Despite facing significant challenges, Volkswagen has demonstrated the importance of crisis management and rebuilding trust. The company's commitment to family governance and its ability to learn from past mistakes have been crucial in its recovery.

- Rana: Rana's success can be attributed to its focus on innovation and expansion. The company's ability to adapt to changing consumer preferences and expand its product offerings has driven its growth in the pasta industry.

- Benetton: Benetton's success lies in its unique approach to fashion, diversity, and social impact. The company's bold and controversial advertising campaigns, combined with its commitment to social responsibility, have made it a global brand.

- Zanussi: Zanussi's success can be attributed to its innovation and adaptability in the home appliance industry. The company's ability to anticipate market trends and develop innovative products has allowed it to stay ahead of the competition.

- Diesel: Diesel's success lies in its creativity, rebellion, and strong brand identity. The company's unique marketing strategies and ability to connect with its target audience have made it a global leader in the fashion industry.

- Luxottica: Luxottica's dominance in the eyewear industry can be attributed to its vertical integration strategy. The company's control over the entire value chain, from design to distribution, has allowed it to maintain a competitive edge.

- Maina: Maina's commitment to tradition, quality, and artisanal excellence has made it a leader in the baking industry. The company's focus on preserving traditional baking techniques while embracing modern technology has set it apart from its competitors.

- Kaiser: Kaiser's success can be attributed to its innovation and expansion strategies in the food industry. The company's ability to identify new market opportunities and adapt its product offerings has driven its growth.

- Esselunga: Esselunga's customer-centric approach has been instrumental in its success in the retail industry. The company's focus on providing exceptional customer service and meeting the needs of its customers has built a loyal customer base.

These successful family companies demonstrate the power of family values, long-term perspective, innovation, and commitment to quality. Other companies can learn from their experiences and apply these principles to their own businesses. By understanding the unique challenges and advantages of family companies, businesses can navigate their own paths to success.

1.2 The Importance of Family Values

Family values play a crucial role in the success of family companies. These values are the guiding principles that shape the company's culture, decision-making processes, and long-term vision.

They provide a strong foundation for the company's growth, sustainability, and ability to navigate challenges. In this section, we will explore the importance of family values in the context of successful family companies and discuss how these values can be applied to other businesses.

1.2.1 Defining Family Values

Family values are the beliefs, principles, and traditions that are passed down through generations within a family. They are deeply rooted in the family's history, culture, and experiences. These values shape the family's identity and serve as a compass for their actions and behaviors.

In the context of family companies, these values extend beyond the family unit and become the driving force behind the company's operations. They influence the company's mission, vision, and overall strategy. Family values often revolve around concepts such as integrity, trust, loyalty, innovation, social responsibility, and long-term thinking.

1.2.2 Alignment with Stakeholders

One of the key advantages of family companies is their ability to align the interests of stakeholders, including family members, employees, customers, and the community. Family values provide a common ground for all stakeholders, fostering a sense of purpose and shared goals.

Family companies often prioritize long-term relationships over short-term gains. They focus on building trust and loyalty with their employees, suppliers, and customers. This emphasis on relationships creates a strong sense of commitment and dedication, leading to higher levels of employee engagement, customer satisfaction, and overall business success.

1.2.3 Continuity and Stability

Family values contribute to the continuity and stability of family companies. These values are deeply ingrained in the family's DNA and are passed down from one generation to the next. They provide a sense of identity and purpose that transcends individual leaders or market trends.

Family companies often have a long-term perspective, driven by their commitment to preserving the family legacy and ensuring the company's sustainability for future generations. This long-term orientation allows them to weather economic downturns, adapt to changing market conditions, and make strategic decisions that prioritize the company's long-term success over short-term gains.

1.2.4 Ethical Decision-Making

Family values serve as a moral compass for family companies, guiding their decision-making processes and ensuring ethical behavior. These values promote transparency, fairness, and accountability in all aspects of the business.

Family companies often prioritize the well-being of their employees, customers, and the environment over maximizing profits. They take a holistic approach to business, considering the social and environmental impact of their actions. This commitment to ethical practices not only enhances the company's reputation but also fosters trust and loyalty among stakeholders.

1.2.5 Flexibility and Adaptability

Family values provide a strong foundation for family companies to navigate challenges and adapt to changing circumstances. These values promote a culture of resilience, innovation, and continuous improvement.

Family companies often have a strong entrepreneurial spirit, driven by their willingness to take calculated risks and embrace change. They encourage creativity and empower employees to contribute their ideas and expertise. This flexibility and adaptability enable family companies to seize opportunities, overcome obstacles, and stay ahead of the competition.

1.2.6 Lessons for Other Companies

The success of family companies offers valuable lessons for other businesses, regardless of their size or sector. By embracing family values, companies can create a strong organizational culture, build trust with stakeholders, and foster long-term sustainability.

Firstly, companies should define their core values and ensure alignment between these values and their business strategies. By clearly articulating their values, companies can create a shared sense of purpose and direction among employees, leading to increased motivation and productivity.

Secondly, companies should prioritize long-term relationships with stakeholders. By investing in building trust and loyalty, companies can create a competitive advantage and enhance their reputation. This includes treating employees with respect, providing excellent customer service, and engaging in socially responsible practices.

Thirdly, companies should adopt an ethical approach to decision-making. By considering the broader impact of their actions, companies can build trust with stakeholders and contribute to a more sustainable and equitable society.

Lastly, companies should foster a culture of flexibility, innovation, and adaptability. By encouraging creativity and empowering employees, companies can stay ahead of the curve and seize opportunities in a rapidly changing business landscape.

In conclusion, family values are a critical component of the success of family companies. These values provide a strong foundation for the company's culture, decision-making processes, and long-term vision. By embracing family values, companies can create a strong organizational culture, build trust with stakeholders, and foster long-term sustainability. The lessons learned from successful family companies can be applied to businesses of all sizes and sectors, enabling them to thrive in an ever-evolving business environment.

1.3 The Unique Challenges of Family Companies

Family companies have a unique set of challenges that they must navigate in order to achieve long-term success. While these challenges can vary depending on the specific company and industry, there are several common themes that emerge when examining the experiences of successful family businesses. In this section, we will explore some of the key challenges that family companies face and how they can overcome them.

1.3.1 Balancing Family and Business Dynamics

One of the most significant challenges for family companies is finding the right balance between family dynamics and business operations. In many cases, family members hold key positions within the company, which can lead to complex interpersonal relationships and potential conflicts of interest. It is crucial for family businesses to establish clear roles and responsibilities for family members, ensuring that decisions are made based on merit and the best interests of the company.

Successful family companies understand the importance of separating family matters from business matters. They establish formal governance structures and professional management practices to ensure transparency, accountability, and fairness. By implementing clear policies and procedures, family businesses can minimize the potential for conflicts and create a more harmonious working environment.

1.3.2 Succession Planning and Leadership Transition

Another significant challenge for family companies is planning for leadership succession and ensuring a smooth transition from one generation to the next. Succession planning involves identifying and preparing the next generation of leaders within the family, which can be a complex and delicate process. It requires careful consideration of the skills, capabilities, and aspirations of family members, as well as the needs of the business.

Successful family companies invest in developing the leadership capabilities of the next generation early on. They provide opportunities for family members to gain experience and knowledge outside of the family business, encouraging them to bring fresh perspectives and ideas back to the company. Additionally, they establish mentorship programs and create a culture of continuous learning to ensure a seamless transition of leadership.

1.3.3 Maintaining a Long-Term Perspective

Family companies often have a long-term perspective that sets them apart from their non-family counterparts. They are driven by a desire to build a lasting legacy and create value for future generations. However, this long-term focus can also present challenges, particularly in industries that are subject to rapid change and disruption.

Successful family companies strike a balance between preserving tradition and embracing innovation. They understand the importance of adapting to changing market conditions and staying ahead of the curve. By fostering a culture of innovation and encouraging entrepreneurial thinking, family businesses can position themselves for long-term success while staying true to their core values and heritage.

1.3.4 Professionalizing the Business

Family companies often start as small, entrepreneurial ventures, with family members wearing multiple hats and taking on various roles within the organization. As the company grows, however, it becomes essential to professionalize the business and bring in outside expertise to support its continued success.

Successful family companies recognize the need to bring in professional managers and executives who can bring fresh perspectives and specialized skills to the table. They understand that professionalization does not mean losing the family's influence or values but rather complementing them with external expertise. By combining the entrepreneurial spirit of the family with the professionalism of outside talent, family businesses can achieve sustainable growth and competitiveness.

1.3.5 Nurturing Family Values and Culture

Family companies often have a strong sense of identity and a unique set of values that have been passed down through generations. These values and culture can be a source of strength and a competitive advantage. However, they can also present challenges when it comes to attracting and retaining non-family employees and adapting to a changing business environment.

Successful family companies understand the importance of nurturing their values and culture while remaining open to new ideas and perspectives. They create a sense of belonging and purpose for all employees, regardless of their family ties, and foster a culture of inclusivity and collaboration. By leveraging their unique heritage and values, family businesses can create a strong brand identity and differentiate themselves in the market.

1.3.6 Building Trust and Reputation

Trust and reputation are critical for the success of any business, but they take on added significance for family companies. The actions and decisions of family members can have a direct impact on the company's reputation and the trust of its stakeholders. Building and maintaining trust requires transparency, integrity, and a commitment to ethical business practices.

Successful family companies prioritize building strong relationships with their stakeholders, including customers, employees, suppliers, and the local community. They communicate openly and honestly, take responsibility for their actions, and demonstrate a genuine commitment to social and environmental responsibility. By consistently delivering on their promises and acting with integrity, family businesses can build a strong reputation and earn the trust of their stakeholders.

In conclusion, family companies face unique challenges that require careful navigation and strategic decision-making. By balancing family and business dynamics, planning for leadership succession, maintaining a long-term perspective, professionalizing the business, nurturing family values and culture, and building trust and reputation, family companies can overcome these challenges and achieve long-term success. Other companies can learn from the experiences of successful family businesses and apply these lessons to their own organizations, regardless of their size or industry.

1.4 The Success Stories of Family Companies

Family companies have a unique dynamic that sets them apart from other businesses. They often have a long-term perspective, a strong sense of purpose, and a commitment to their core values. In this section, we will explore the success stories of 13 different family companies and uncover the secrets behind their achievements. These companies span various sectors, sizes, and leadership styles, providing valuable insights for other businesses looking to thrive in today's competitive landscape.

1.4.1 IKEA: Building a Global Empire

IKEA, founded by Ingvar Kamprad, is a prime example of a family company that has achieved global success. The company's success can be attributed to its unique business model, which focuses on offering affordable, well-designed furniture to the masses. IKEA's flat-pack concept and self-assembly approach have revolutionized the furniture industry, allowing the company to expand rapidly and establish a strong global presence. The involvement of the Kamprad family in the company's operations has played a crucial role in maintaining its core values and ensuring its long-term success.

1.4.2 Toyota: The Power of Continuous Improvement

Toyota, a Japanese automotive manufacturer, is renowned for its commitment to continuous improvement and quality. The company's success can be attributed to the Toyota Production System, which emphasizes eliminating waste, empowering employees, and fostering a culture of innovation. The Toyota family's involvement in the company has helped maintain a long-term perspective and a focus on sustainable growth. Other companies can learn from Toyota's emphasis on quality, efficiency, and employee empowerment to drive their own success.

1.4.3 Ferrero: Innovation and Tradition

Ferrero, a family-owned Italian confectionery company, has achieved remarkable success through a combination of innovation and tradition. The company's commitment to product excellence and continuous innovation has allowed it to create iconic brands such as Nutella and Kinder. Ferrero's ability to balance tradition with modernity has been a key factor in its success. By staying true to its core values and embracing new technologies and consumer trends, Ferrero has been able to maintain its position as a leader in the confectionery industry.

1.4.4 Patagonia: Environmental Responsibility and Ethical Leadership

Patagonia, an outdoor clothing and gear company, has built its success on a strong commitment to environmental responsibility and ethical leadership. The company's founder, Yvon Chouinard, instilled a deep sense of environmental stewardship within the organization. Patagonia's dedication to sustainability, transparency, and social responsibility has resonated with consumers and helped the company thrive in a competitive market. Other companies can learn from Patagonia's focus on purpose-driven business practices and the integration of sustainability into their core strategies.

1.4.5 Volkswagen: Navigating Challenges and Rebuilding Trust

Volkswagen, a German automotive manufacturer, faced a significant crisis in 2015 when it was revealed that the company had manipulated emissions tests. However, the company's ability to navigate this crisis and rebuild trust can serve as a valuable lesson for other businesses. The involvement of the Volkswagen family in the company's governance and decision-making processes has played a crucial role in its recovery. By taking responsibility, implementing changes, and prioritizing transparency, Volkswagen has been able to regain the trust of its customers and stakeholders.

1.4.6 Rana: From Small Business to Pasta Empire

Rana, an Italian pasta company, started as a small family business and has grown into a global pasta empire. The company's success can be attributed to its focus on innovation, quality, and expansion. Rana's ability to adapt to changing consumer preferences and expand into new markets has been instrumental in its growth. The family's involvement in the business has allowed them to maintain a strong connection to their heritage and ensure the quality and authenticity of their products.

1.4.7 Benetton: Fashion, Diversity, and Social Impact

Benetton, an Italian fashion brand, has made a name for itself through its unique approach to fashion, diversity, and social impact. The company's commitment to inclusivity and social responsibility has set it apart from its competitors. Benetton's family legacy and involvement in the business have helped shape its brand identity and values. By leveraging the power of diversity and addressing social issues, Benetton has been able to create a strong brand that resonates with consumers worldwide.

1.4.8 Zanussi: Innovation and Adaptability in the Home Appliance Industry

Zanussi, an Italian home appliance manufacturer, has achieved success through its focus on innovation and adaptability. The company's ability to anticipate and respond to changing consumer needs has allowed it to stay ahead in a highly competitive industry. Zanussi's family values, including a commitment to quality and customer satisfaction, have been integral to its success. Other companies can learn from Zanussi's emphasis on innovation, adaptability, and customer-centricity to drive their own growth.

1.4.9 Diesel: Creativity, Rebellion, and Brand Identity

Diesel, an Italian fashion brand, has built its success on a unique brand identity that embraces creativity and rebellion. The company's founder, Renzo Rosso, infused Diesel with a sense of individuality and non-conformity. Diesel's family influence has allowed the company to maintain its rebellious spirit and stay true to its core values. By embracing unconventional marketing strategies and fostering a culture of creativity, Diesel has been able to differentiate itself in the fashion industry.

1.4.10 Luxottica: Eyewear Dominance and Vertical Integration

Luxottica, an Italian eyewear company, has achieved dominance in the industry through its vertical integration strategy. The company controls every aspect of its supply chain, from design and manufacturing to distribution and retail. Luxottica's family values, including a focus on quality and craftsmanship, have been instrumental in its success. Other companies can learn from Luxottica's vertical integration approach and commitment to excellence to create a competitive advantage in their respective industries.

1.4.11 Maina: Tradition, Quality, and Artisanal Excellence

Maina, an Italian bakery company, has thrived by embracing tradition, quality, and artisanal excellence. The company's commitment to using traditional baking methods and high-quality ingredients has allowed it to create exceptional products. Maina's family involvement in the business has helped preserve its heritage and ensure the consistency and authenticity of its offerings. By staying true to its roots and focusing on craftsmanship, Maina has been able to establish itself as a leader in the bakery industry.

1.4.12 Kaiser: Innovation and Expansion in the Food Industry

Kaiser, a family-owned food company, has achieved success through its focus on innovation and expansion. The company's ability to identify emerging trends and develop innovative food products has allowed it to stay ahead in a rapidly changing industry. Kaiser's family values, including a commitment to quality and customer satisfaction, have been key drivers of its growth. Other companies can learn from Kaiser's emphasis on innovation, adaptability, and customer-centricity to drive their own success in the food industry.

1.4.13 Esselunga: Customer Focus and Retail Success

Esselunga, an Italian supermarket chain, has achieved retail success through its unwavering focus on customer satisfaction. The company's commitment to providing high-quality products, exceptional service, and a pleasant shopping experience has earned it a loyal customer base. Esselunga's family legacy and involvement in the business have helped shape its customer-centric approach. By prioritizing customer needs and continuously improving its offerings, Esselunga has been able to thrive in a competitive market.

These success stories of family companies demonstrate the power of long-term vision, commitment to core values, innovation, and adaptability. By learning from their experiences, other companies can gain valuable insights and apply these principles to their own businesses. Whether it is embracing sustainability, empowering employees, or focusing on customer satisfaction, the secrets of these successful family companies can inspire and guide others on their path to success.

IKEA

2.1 The History and Origins of IKEA

IKEA, one of the most successful family companies in the world, has a fascinating history that has shaped its growth and success. Founded in 1943 by Ingvar Kamprad, a young entrepreneur from Sweden, IKEA has become a global empire in the furniture and home goods industry. The story of IKEA's origins is not only inspiring but also provides valuable insights into the strategies and principles that have propelled the company to its current status.

Ingvar Kamprad's entrepreneurial journey began at a young age. Growing up in rural Sweden, he developed a keen interest in business and started selling matches to his neighbors at the age of five. This early experience taught him the importance of hard work, frugality, and the value of money. These principles would later become the foundation of IKEA's success.

In 1943, at the age of 17, Kamprad founded IKEA as a mail-order business, initially selling a variety of products such as pens, wallets, and picture frames. The name IKEA is an acronym derived from Kamprad's initials (I.K.) and the first letters of the farm and village where he grew up (Elmtaryd and Agunnaryd). The company's focus on affordability and functionality was evident from the beginning, as Kamprad aimed to provide quality products at affordable prices to the masses.

The turning point for IKEA came in the late 1940s when Kamprad introduced furniture into the company's product range. He recognized the potential in the post-war market, where people were in need of affordable and well-designed furniture. Kamprad's vision was to create furniture that was not only functional but also aesthetically pleasing, challenging the notion that good design was only accessible to the wealthy.

To keep prices low, Kamprad implemented innovative strategies such as flat-packaging and self-assembly. By designing furniture that could be easily transported and assembled by customers themselves, IKEA was able to reduce manufacturing and transportation costs significantly. This approach also aligned with Kamprad's belief in empowering customers and involving them in the creation process.

IKEA's first showroom opened in 1953 in Älmhult, Sweden, and quickly gained popularity. The showroom allowed customers to experience the furniture in a real-life setting, showcasing the company's commitment to creating functional and stylish living spaces. This concept of the showroom, combined with the affordability and quality of IKEA's products, became the cornerstone of the company's success.

As IKEA expanded internationally, it faced various challenges, including cultural differences, market saturation, and competition. However, the company's commitment to its core values and principles remained unwavering. Family involvement has played a crucial role in IKEA's success, with Kamprad's three sons, Peter, Jonas, and

Mathias, taking on leadership roles within the company.

The family's commitment to the long-term success of IKEA is evident in their approach to corporate governance. They have established a unique ownership structure that ensures the company's independence and allows for strategic decision-making. This structure, combined with a strong focus on sustainability and social responsibility, has helped IKEA maintain its position as a global leader in the industry.

IKEA's success can be attributed to several key factors. Firstly, the company's ability to understand and meet the needs of its customers has been crucial. By offering affordable, well-designed, and functional products, IKEA has been able to appeal to a wide range of consumers. Secondly, IKEA's commitment to innovation and continuous improvement has allowed the company to stay ahead of the competition. From product design to supply chain management, IKEA constantly seeks ways to improve efficiency and sustainability.

Furthermore, IKEA's strong company culture, rooted in its Swedish heritage, has fostered a sense of unity and shared values among its employees. The company's emphasis on teamwork, open communication, and a flat organizational structure has created an environment where creativity and collaboration thrive.

Other companies can learn valuable lessons from IKEA's success. Firstly, understanding and meeting customer needs should be a top priority. By offering products and services that provide value and address customer pain points, companies can build a loyal customer base. Secondly, embracing innovation and continuously improving processes is essential for long-term success. Companies should constantly seek ways to enhance their products, services, and operations to stay relevant in a rapidly changing business landscape.

Additionally, fostering a strong company culture that aligns with the company's values and goals is crucial. A positive and inclusive work environment can lead to increased employee satisfaction, productivity, and innovation. Finally, family involvement can bring unique advantages to a company. Family businesses often have a long-term perspective and a strong commitment to the company's success, which can be a significant asset in navigating challenges and driving growth.

In conclusion, the history and origins of IKEA provide valuable insights into the strategies and principles that have contributed to its success. From its humble beginnings as a mail-order business to its current status as a global furniture empire, IKEA's commitment to affordability, functionality, innovation, and sustainability has set it apart from its competitors. Other companies can learn from IKEA's customer-centric approach, focus on continuous improvement, strong company culture, and the advantages of family involvement. By applying these lessons, companies can strive for long-term success and make a positive impact in their respective industries.

2.2 The IKEA Business Model

IKEA is a global household name known for its affordable and stylish furniture. The company's success can be attributed to its unique business model, which combines innovative design, cost-effective production, and a strong focus on customer experience. Understanding the IKEA business model can provide valuable insights for other companies looking to achieve success in their respective industries.

2.2.1 The Concept of Flat-Pack Furniture

One of the key elements of the IKEA business model is the concept of flat-pack furniture. Instead of selling fully assembled furniture, IKEA offers products that can be easily transported and assembled by the customers themselves. This approach allows IKEA to reduce production and transportation costs significantly, making their products more affordable for a wider customer base.

The flat-pack concept also enables IKEA to optimize its supply chain and distribution network. By packaging products efficiently, IKEA can transport more items in a single shipment, reducing transportation costs and minimizing environmental impact. This approach has helped IKEA expand its global presence and reach customers in various parts of the world.

2.2.2 Emphasis on Scandinavian Design and Functionality

IKEA's success can also be attributed to its emphasis on Scandinavian design and functionality. The company's furniture and home accessories are known for their clean lines, simplicity, and practicality. This design philosophy resonates with customers who appreciate minimalist aesthetics and functional solutions for their homes.

By focusing on Scandinavian design principles, IKEA has created a distinct brand identity that sets it apart from competitors. The company's products are often associated with modernity, affordability, and practicality. This design-driven approach has helped IKEA build a loyal customer base and establish itself as a leader in the furniture industry.

2.2.3 Integration of In-Store Experience and E-Commerce

IKEA understands the importance of providing a seamless shopping experience for its customers. The company has successfully integrated its physical stores with its e-commerce platform, allowing customers to browse and purchase products both online and offline. This omnichannel approach ensures that customers can choose the most convenient way to shop, whether it's visiting a store or making a purchase from the comfort of their homes.

IKEA's physical stores are designed to provide an immersive and interactive experience for customers. They feature room displays, where customers can visualize how IKEA products can be incorporated into their own homes. Additionally, the stores often include restaurants and play areas for children, creating a welcoming and family-friendly environment.

2.2.4 Commitment to Sustainability and Social Responsibility

Another aspect of the IKEA business model is its commitment to sustainability and social responsibility. The company has implemented various initiatives to reduce its environmental impact, such as using renewable energy, promoting recycling, and sourcing materials responsibly. IKEA also strives to create a positive social impact by supporting local communities and providing fair working conditions for its employees.

By aligning its business practices with sustainability and social responsibility, IKEA has gained the trust and loyalty of environmentally conscious customers. This commitment to ethical and responsible practices has not only enhanced the company's reputation but also contributed to its long-term success.

2.2.5 Lessons for Other Companies

The IKEA business model offers several valuable lessons for other companies:

1. **Innovation and Cost Efficiency**: By embracing innovative approaches like flat-pack furniture, companies can reduce costs, optimize their supply chains, and offer affordable products to a wider customer base.

2. **Design and Branding**: Investing in design and branding can help companies differentiate themselves from competitors and create a strong brand identity that resonates with customers.

3. **Omnichannel Strategy**: Integrating physical stores with e-commerce platforms allows companies to provide a seamless shopping experience and cater to the preferences of different customer segments.

4. **Sustainability and Social Responsibility**: Incorporating sustainable and socially responsible practices into business operations can enhance a company's reputation, attract environmentally conscious customers, and contribute to long-term success.

5. **Customer-Centric Approach**: Creating an immersive and interactive in-store experience, as well as prioritizing customer convenience and satisfaction, can build customer loyalty and drive business growth.

By studying the success of IKEA and other family companies, businesses can gain valuable insights and apply these lessons to their own operations. The power of family companies lies not only in their unique business models but also in their ability to adapt, innovate, and prioritize the needs of their customers and communities.

2.3 Family Involvement in IKEA's Success

Family involvement has played a crucial role in the success of IKEA, one of the world's largest furniture retailers. Founded in 1943 by Ingvar Kamprad, IKEA has grown from a small mail-order business to a global empire with over 400 stores in more than 50 countries. The company's unique business model and commitment to family values have been key factors in its remarkable growth and sustained success.

2.3.1 The Kamprad Family Legacy

The Kamprad family has been instrumental in shaping IKEA's culture and business strategy. Ingvar Kamprad, the founder of IKEA, instilled his entrepreneurial spirit and frugal mindset into the company's DNA. He believed in the power of simplicity, affordability, and functionality in furniture design, which became the cornerstone of IKEA's success.

Ingvar Kamprad's three sons, Peter, Jonas, and Mathias, have also played significant roles in the company. They have been involved in various aspects of IKEA's operations, including product development, marketing, and sustainability initiatives. The Kamprad family's long-term commitment to the company has provided stability and continuity, allowing IKEA to navigate through challenges and pursue ambitious growth strategies.

2.3.2 Family Values in IKEA's Corporate Culture

Family values are deeply ingrained in IKEA's corporate culture. The company places a strong emphasis on creating a sense of belonging and togetherness among its employees, often referred to as "IKEA family." This inclusive culture fosters a collaborative and supportive work environment, where individuals are encouraged to contribute their ideas and talents.

IKEA's commitment to family values extends beyond its employees. The company also prioritizes the well-being of its customers and the communities it operates in. IKEA's products are designed with the needs and aspirations of families in mind, offering practical solutions for everyday living. Additionally, IKEA actively engages in social and environmental initiatives, such as promoting sustainable sourcing and supporting local communities.

2.3.3 Family Governance and Succession Planning

Effective family governance and succession planning have been critical in ensuring IKEA's long-term success. The Kamprad family has implemented a structured governance framework that outlines the roles, responsibilities, and decision-making processes within the family and the company. This framework helps maintain a balance between family interests and the best interests of the business.

IKEA has also implemented a robust succession planning process to ensure a smooth transition of leadership from one generation to the next. The Kamprad family has actively involved the next generation in the company's operations and decision-making, preparing them to take on leadership roles in the future. This deliberate approach to succession planning has helped IKEA maintain its entrepreneurial spirit and innovative mindset over the years.

2.3.4 Long-Term Perspective and Innovation

Family involvement in IKEA has allowed the company to take a long-term perspective and prioritize innovation. Unlike publicly traded companies driven by short-term financial goals, IKEA can focus on investing in research and development, sustainable practices, and long-term growth strategies without the pressure of quarterly earnings reports.

The Kamprad family's commitment to innovation is evident in IKEA's product offerings and business model. The company continuously seeks new ways to improve its products, processes, and customer experience. From flat-pack furniture to self-service shopping, IKEA has revolutionized the furniture industry by introducing innovative concepts that have resonated with consumers worldwide.

2.3.5 Lessons Learned from IKEA

Other companies can learn valuable lessons from IKEA's success and family involvement:

1. **Embrace simplicity and affordability:** IKEA's success lies in its ability to offer well-designed, functional products at affordable prices. Companies should strive to simplify their offerings and make them accessible to a wide range of customers.

2. **Cultivate a strong corporate culture:** By fostering a sense of belonging and togetherness, companies can create a positive work environment that encourages collaboration and innovation.

3. **Prioritize long-term goals:** Companies should focus on long-term growth and sustainability, rather than being solely driven by short-term financial gains. This allows for

investment in innovation and strategic initiatives.

4. **Implement effective family governance:** Family businesses should establish clear governance structures and succession plans to ensure a smooth transition of leadership and balance family interests with business objectives.

5. **Embrace innovation:** Companies should continuously seek new ways to improve their products, processes, and customer experience. Innovation can be a key driver of success and differentiation in the market.

By studying the success of IKEA and other family companies, businesses can gain insights into the power of family involvement, the importance of long-term thinking, and the value of embracing innovation and family values in their own operations.

2.4 Lessons Learned from IKEA

IKEA, the Swedish furniture giant, has become a global empire with its unique business model and family involvement. Through its success, there are several valuable lessons that other companies can learn from IKEA's journey.

2.4.1 Embrace Simplicity and Affordability

One of the key lessons from IKEA's success is the importance of embracing simplicity and affordability. IKEA revolutionized the furniture industry by offering well-designed, functional products at affordable prices. They focused on providing value to customers without compromising on quality. This approach allowed them to tap into a wider customer base and attract a large number of loyal customers.

Other companies can learn from IKEA's emphasis on simplicity and affordability by understanding the needs and preferences of their target market. By offering products or services that are accessible and reasonably priced, companies can attract a larger customer base and build brand loyalty.

2.4.2 Design for Functionality and Practicality

IKEA's success can also be attributed to its focus on designing products that are functional and practical. Their furniture and home accessories are designed with the needs of everyday life in mind. IKEA's products are known for their smart storage solutions, modular designs, and easy assembly, making them highly convenient for customers.

Companies can learn from IKEA's approach by prioritizing functionality and practicality in their product design. By understanding the pain points and challenges faced by their customers, companies can create products that provide solutions and enhance the overall user experience.

2.4.3 Create an Engaging Customer Experience

IKEA has mastered the art of creating an engaging customer experience. Their stores are designed as immersive environments, allowing customers to explore and interact with the products. IKEA's showrooms provide inspiration and ideas for customers to envision how the products can be incorporated into their own homes.

Other companies can learn from IKEA's approach by focusing on creating memorable and immersive experiences for their customers. By designing physical or digital spaces that engage and inspire, companies can enhance customer satisfaction and build long-term relationships.

2.4.4 Emphasize Sustainability and Social Responsibility

IKEA has made significant efforts to incorporate sustainability and social responsibility into its business practices. They have committed to using renewable materials, reducing waste, and promoting fair labor practices. IKEA's sustainability initiatives have not only helped the environment but have also resonated with customers who value ethical and responsible business practices.

Companies can learn from IKEA's emphasis on sustainability by integrating environmentally friendly practices into their operations. By adopting sustainable sourcing, reducing waste, and supporting social causes, companies can enhance their brand reputation and attract socially conscious customers.

2.4.5 Foster a Strong Company Culture

IKEA's success can be attributed, in part, to its strong company culture. The company values teamwork, simplicity, and a down-to-earth approach. IKEA's founder, Ingvar Kamprad, instilled a sense of frugality and humility within the organization, which has been carried forward by subsequent generations of the family.

Other companies can learn from IKEA's focus on fostering a strong company culture. By defining and promoting core values, companies can create a sense of purpose and unity among employees. A strong company culture can drive employee engagement, innovation, and ultimately, business success.

2.4.6 Embrace Family Involvement and Long-Term Vision

Family involvement has played a crucial role in IKEA's success. The Kamprad family has maintained control over the company, allowing them to make long-term strategic decisions and maintain the company's vision. This continuity has enabled IKEA to stay true to its core values and maintain a consistent brand identity.

Other companies can learn from IKEA's approach by recognizing the value of family involvement and long-term vision. By involving family members in leadership roles and embracing a long-term perspective, companies can ensure continuity, stability, and a strong sense of purpose.

2.4.7 Adapt to Changing Market Trends

IKEA has demonstrated the ability to adapt to changing market trends. They have expanded their product range, embraced e-commerce, and explored new markets to stay relevant and meet the evolving needs of customers. IKEA's ability to anticipate and respond to market changes has been instrumental in its continued success.

Companies can learn from IKEA's agility and adaptability by staying attuned to market trends and customer preferences. By being open to innovation, embracing new technologies, and continuously evolving, companies can remain competitive in a rapidly changing business landscape.

2.4.8 Invest in Employee Development and Well-being

IKEA recognizes the importance of investing in its employees' development and well-being. They provide training and development opportunities, promote a healthy work-life balance, and offer competitive benefits. IKEA's focus on employee satisfaction and well-being has contributed to a positive work culture and high employee retention rates.

Other companies can learn from IKEA's emphasis on employee development and well-being. By investing in their employees' growth, providing a supportive work environment, and recognizing their contributions, companies can foster a motivated and engaged workforce.

In conclusion, IKEA's success can be attributed to its emphasis on simplicity, affordability, functionality, and sustainability. Other companies can learn from IKEA's journey by embracing these principles, creating engaging customer experiences, fostering a strong company culture, and adapting to changing market trends. By incorporating these lessons into their own strategies, companies can increase their chances of long-term success and growth.

Toyota

3.1 The Toyota Philosophy

Toyota, one of the world's largest automobile manufacturers, has achieved remarkable success over the years. The company's philosophy, known as the Toyota Way, has played a significant role in its growth and dominance in the industry. This section will explore the key principles of the Toyota Philosophy and how they have contributed to the company's success.

3.1.1 The Foundation of the Toyota Philosophy

At the core of the Toyota Philosophy is the belief in continuous improvement, also known as Kaizen. This principle emphasizes the importance of constantly seeking ways to improve processes, products, and services. Toyota understands that innovation and progress are not achieved through sporadic bursts of improvement but through a sustained commitment to incremental advancements.

3.1.2 Respect for People

Another fundamental aspect of the Toyota Philosophy is the respect for people. Toyota recognizes that its success is not solely dependent on its products but also on the individuals who contribute to the company's operations. This principle extends beyond the employees to include suppliers, customers, and the community at large. By fostering a culture of respect, Toyota creates an environment that encourages collaboration, creativity, and loyalty.

3.1.3 Just-in-Time Production

Toyota revolutionized the manufacturing industry with its innovative approach to production known as Just-in-Time (JIT). This methodology aims to eliminate waste by producing and delivering products precisely when they are needed. By minimizing inventory and reducing lead times, Toyota can respond quickly to customer demands while maintaining efficiency and cost-effectiveness.

3.1.4 Total Quality Management

Quality is a cornerstone of the Toyota Philosophy. The company is committed to delivering products and services that meet or exceed customer expectations. Toyota's approach to quality management involves empowering employees to take ownership of their work and continuously strive for excellence. By implementing rigorous quality control measures and fostering a culture of accountability, Toyota ensures that every aspect of its operations is focused on delivering superior quality.

3.1.5 The Role of Family in Toyota's Success

Family plays a significant role in Toyota's success and longevity. The company was founded by the Toyoda family, and their values and vision have shaped the organization's culture and direction. The Toyoda family's commitment to innovation, integrity, and long-term thinking has been passed down through generations, creating a strong foundation for the company's continued growth.

3.1.6 Lessons for Other Companies

The success of Toyota and its philosophy holds valuable lessons for other companies, regardless of their sector, size, or leadership structure.

Firstly, the commitment to continuous improvement is crucial. Companies should embrace the idea that there is always room for improvement and encourage their employees to seek innovative solutions and challenge the status quo. By fostering a culture of continuous improvement, companies can stay ahead of the competition and adapt to changing market dynamics.

Secondly, the importance of respecting people cannot be overstated. Companies should prioritize the well-being and development of their employees, suppliers, customers, and the communities they operate in. By creating a culture of respect and collaboration, companies can build strong relationships, enhance employee engagement, and foster loyalty among stakeholders.

Thirdly, adopting lean manufacturing principles, such as Just-in-Time production, can help companies reduce waste, improve efficiency, and enhance customer satisfaction. By streamlining processes and eliminating unnecessary inventory, companies can respond quickly to customer demands and optimize their operations.

Lastly, a relentless focus on quality is essential for long-term success. Companies should strive to deliver products and services that consistently meet or exceed customer expectations. By implementing robust quality control measures and empowering employees to take ownership of their work, companies can build a reputation for excellence and customer satisfaction.

In conclusion, the Toyota Philosophy has been instrumental in the success of the company. The principles of continuous improvement, respect for people, just-in-time production, and total quality management have set Toyota apart in the automotive industry. Other companies can learn from Toyota's philosophy by embracing a culture of continuous improvement, prioritizing respect for people, adopting lean manufacturing principles, and maintaining a relentless focus on quality. By incorporating these principles into their operations, companies can enhance their competitiveness, drive innovation, and achieve sustainable growth.

3.2 Family Influence in Toyota's Success

Family influence plays a significant role in the success of Toyota, one of the world's leading automobile manufacturers. The Toyota family's commitment to their company's values and long-term vision has been instrumental in shaping the company's culture, innovation, and continuous improvement.

3.2.1 The Toyota Family Legacy

The Toyota family's involvement in the company dates back to its inception in 1937. The founder, Kiichiro Toyoda, established a strong foundation based on the principles of quality, innovation, and customer satisfaction. These values were passed down through generations, creating a legacy that continues to drive Toyota's success.

The family's deep understanding of the company's history, culture, and values has allowed them to maintain a long-term perspective, focusing on sustainable growth rather than short-term gains. This commitment to the company's core principles has been a driving force behind Toyota's ability to adapt and thrive in a rapidly changing industry.

3.2.2 Family Values in Toyota's Business Strategy

Family values are deeply ingrained in Toyota's business strategy. The Toyota family believes in fostering a sense of unity, respect, and loyalty among employees, suppliers, and customers. This emphasis on strong relationships has created a culture of collaboration and trust within the company.

Toyota's family-oriented approach extends beyond its internal operations. The company values its relationships with suppliers, treating them as partners rather than mere vendors. This collaborative approach has allowed Toyota to build long-term, mutually beneficial relationships, ensuring a stable supply chain and high-quality products.

Furthermore, the Toyota family's commitment to social responsibility is evident in their emphasis on environmental sustainability. Toyota has been a pioneer in developing hybrid and electric vehicles, aiming to reduce carbon emissions and promote a greener future. This commitment to sustainability aligns with the family's values and has helped Toyota establish itself as an industry leader in eco-friendly transportation.

3.2.3 Family Involvement in Toyota's Leadership

Family involvement in Toyota's leadership has been a key factor in the company's success. The family's deep understanding of the business and its long-term vision has allowed them to make strategic decisions that prioritize the company's growth and sustainability.

The Toyota family's leadership style is characterized by a focus on consensus-building and a commitment to continuous improvement. They encourage open communication and value input from employees at all levels of the organization. This inclusive approach fosters a culture of innovation and empowers employees to contribute their ideas and expertise.

The family's involvement in Toyota's leadership also ensures stability and continuity. Rather than succumbing to short-term market pressures, the family's long-term perspective allows them to make decisions that prioritize the company's long-term success. This stability has been crucial in navigating challenges and maintaining Toyota's position as a global leader in the automotive industry.

3.2.4 Lessons Learned from Toyota's Success

Other companies can learn valuable lessons from Toyota's success and the family's influence on its achievements:

1. **Long-term vision**: Emphasize the importance of a long-term vision and values

that guide decision-making, even in the face of short-term challenges.

2. **Family values**: Foster a culture of unity, respect, and loyalty within the organization, promoting strong relationships with employees, suppliers, and customers.

3. **Collaboration and trust**: Build collaborative relationships with suppliers, treating them as partners rather than transactional entities, to ensure a stable supply chain and high-quality products.

4. **Social responsibility**: Incorporate environmental sustainability into business strategies, aligning company values with initiatives that promote a greener future.

5. **Inclusive leadership**: Encourage open communication and value input from employees at all levels, fostering a culture of innovation and continuous improvement.

6. **Stability and continuity**: Maintain a long-term perspective in decision-making, prioritizing the company's long-term success over short-term gains.

By embracing these lessons, companies can strive for sustainable growth, foster innovation, and build strong relationships with stakeholders, ultimately positioning themselves for long-term success in their respective industries.

3.3 Toyota's Commitment to Quality

Toyota is a renowned Japanese automotive manufacturer that has become synonymous with quality and reliability. One of the key factors behind Toyota's success is its unwavering commitment to producing vehicles of the highest quality. This commitment to quality has not only helped Toyota build a strong reputation but has also contributed to its long-term success and customer loyalty.

3.3.1 The Toyota Production System

At the heart of Toyota's commitment to quality is the Toyota Production System (TPS). TPS is a unique manufacturing philosophy that focuses on eliminating waste, improving efficiency, and continuously improving processes. It is based on the principles of "Just-in-Time" production and "Kaizen" (continuous improvement).

The "Just-in-Time" principle aims to minimize inventory and reduce waste by producing only what is needed, when it is needed, and in the required quantity. This approach helps Toyota avoid overproduction, which can lead to excess inventory and increased costs.

The "Kaizen" principle emphasizes the importance of continuous improvement in all aspects of the production process. Toyota encourages its employees to identify and address problems, no matter how small, to ensure that quality is consistently improved. This commitment to continuous improvement has allowed Toyota to stay ahead of its competitors and deliver high-quality vehicles to its customers.

3.3.2 Total Quality Management

Toyota's commitment to quality extends beyond the production process. The company has implemented a comprehensive Total Quality Management (TQM) system that involves every aspect of its operations. TQM focuses on meeting customer expectations and continuously improving the quality of products and services.

Toyota places a strong emphasis on customer feedback and uses it to drive improvements in its products and processes. By actively listening to its customers and addressing their concerns, Toyota ensures that its vehicles meet the highest standards of quality and reliability.

3.3.3 Continuous Training and Development

To maintain its commitment to quality, Toyota invests heavily in the training and development of its employees. The company believes that well-trained and motivated employees are essential for delivering high-quality products and services.

Toyota provides extensive training programs to its employees at all levels, from assembly line workers to managers. These programs focus on developing technical skills, problem-solving abilities, and a deep understanding of the Toyota Production System. By equipping its employees with the necessary knowledge and skills, Toyota ensures that quality is ingrained in every aspect of its operations.

Toyota recognizes the importance of strong relationships with its suppliers in maintaining quality standards. The company works closely with its suppliers to ensure that they meet Toyota's stringent quality requirements.

Toyota collaborates with its suppliers from the early stages of product development, providing them with the necessary support and guidance to meet its quality standards. This collaborative approach helps Toyota build a network of reliable suppliers who share its commitment to quality.

3.3.5 Lessons for Other Companies

Other companies can learn valuable lessons from Toyota's commitment to quality. Here are some key takeaways:

1. **Continuous Improvement**: Embrace the philosophy of continuous improvement and encourage employees to identify and address quality issues proactively.

2. **Customer Focus**: Place a strong emphasis on understanding and meeting customer expectations. Actively seek customer feedback and use it to drive improvements in products and services.

3. **Training and Development**: Invest in the training and development of employees to ensure they have the necessary skills and knowledge to deliver high-quality products and services.

4. **Supplier Collaboration**: Build strong relationships with suppliers and collaborate closely with them to ensure they meet the company's quality standards.

5. **Total Quality Management**: Implement a comprehensive quality management system that involves every aspect of the company's operations. Focus on continuously improving processes and meeting customer expectations.

By adopting these principles and practices, companies can enhance their commitment to quality and improve their overall performance. Toyota's success serves as a testament to the power of a strong commitment to quality and continuous improvement in achieving long-term success in any industry.

3.4 Applying Toyota's Principles to Other Companies

Toyota is widely recognized as one of the most successful and innovative companies in the world. Its principles and practices have not only revolutionized the automotive industry but have also inspired and influenced companies across various sectors. In this section, we will explore how other companies can apply Toyota's principles to enhance their own success.

3.4.1 Embracing Continuous Improvement

One of the key principles that sets Toyota apart is its commitment to continuous improvement, also known as Kaizen. This philosophy emphasizes the importance of constantly seeking ways to improve processes, products, and services. Companies in any industry can benefit from adopting this mindset.

To apply Toyota's principle of continuous improvement, organizations should encourage a culture of innovation and learning. This involves empowering employees at all levels to identify and suggest improvements, fostering a sense of ownership and accountability. Regular feedback loops and open communication channels should be established to facilitate the exchange of ideas and ensure that improvements are implemented effectively.

3.4.2 Building Strong Supplier Relationships

Toyota's success can also be attributed to its strong relationships with suppliers. The company recognizes that suppliers play a crucial role in delivering high-quality products and services to customers. Other companies can learn from Toyota's approach by prioritizing collaboration and long-term partnerships with their suppliers.

To apply Toyota's supplier relationship principles, companies should focus on building trust, transparency, and mutual respect. This involves establishing clear expectations, providing support and training, and fostering open lines of communication. By working closely with suppliers, companies can enhance efficiency, reduce costs, and improve overall product quality.

3.4.3 Prioritizing Quality and Customer Satisfaction

Toyota's commitment to quality is legendary. The company places a strong emphasis on delivering products and services that meet or exceed customer expectations. This dedication to quality has earned Toyota a reputation for reliability and customer satisfaction. Other companies can learn from Toyota's focus on quality and customer-centricity.

To apply Toyota's principles of quality and customer satisfaction, companies should prioritize understanding their customers' needs and preferences. This involves conducting market research, gathering customer feedback, and using data-driven insights to drive product development and improvement. By consistently delivering high-quality products and exceptional customer service, companies can build strong customer loyalty and gain a competitive edge.

3.4.4 Empowering Employees and Promoting a Culture of Respect

Toyota's success is also attributed to its strong focus on employee empowerment and fostering a culture of respect. The company values its employees as its most valuable asset and recognizes that their skills, knowledge, and dedication are essential to achieving organizational goals. Other companies can learn from Toyota's approach to employee engagement and empowerment.

To apply Toyota's principles of employee empowerment and respect, companies should invest in their employees' development and well-being. This involves providing training opportunities, promoting a healthy work-life balance, and creating a supportive and inclusive work environment. By empowering employees and valuing their contributions, companies can foster a culture of innovation, collaboration, and continuous improvement.

3.4.5 Implementing Lean Manufacturing and Waste Reduction

Toyota is renowned for its lean manufacturing principles, which aim to eliminate waste and maximize efficiency. The company's approach focuses on identifying and eliminating non-value-added activities, reducing inventory, and optimizing production processes. Other companies can learn from Toyota's lean manufacturing practices to improve their own operational efficiency.

To apply Toyota's lean manufacturing principles, companies should conduct thorough process analyses to identify areas of waste and inefficiency. By implementing lean tools and techniques such as value stream mapping, just-in-time production, and continuous flow, companies can streamline their operations, reduce costs, and improve overall productivity.

3.4.6 Embracing a Long-Term Perspective

Toyota's success can also be attributed to its long-term perspective and commitment to sustainable growth. The company prioritizes long-term value creation over short-term gains, focusing on building enduring relationships with customers, suppliers, and other stakeholders. Other companies can learn from Toyota's approach to long-term thinking and sustainability.

To apply Toyota's long-term perspective, companies should develop a clear vision and mission that aligns with their core values. This involves setting realistic goals, investing in research and development, and making strategic decisions that prioritize long-term sustainability. By taking a holistic approach to business and considering the impact of their actions on all stakeholders, companies can build a strong foundation for long-term success.

In conclusion, Toyota's principles and practices have proven to be highly effective in driving success and innovation. By embracing continuous improvement, building strong supplier relationships, prioritizing quality and customer satisfaction, empowering employees, implementing lean manufacturing, and embracing a long-term perspective, companies in any industry can learn valuable lessons from Toyota's success and apply them to enhance their own performance.

Ferrero

4.1 The Ferrero Family Legacy

The Ferrero family has left an indelible mark on the confectionery industry with their innovative products and unwavering commitment to quality. The story of Ferrero is a testament to the power of family values and the ability to balance tradition with modernity.

4.1.1 A Sweet Beginning

The Ferrero family's journey began in 1946 when Pietro Ferrero, a pastry maker from Italy, created a hazelnut and cocoa spread known as Nutella. This revolutionary product quickly gained popularity and laid the foundation for the Ferrero brand. Pietro's son, Michele Ferrero, took over the business and expanded its product line, introducing iconic treats such as Ferrero Rocher and Kinder Chocolate.

4.1.2 Family Values at the Core

One of the key factors behind Ferrero's success is the strong emphasis on family values. The Ferrero family has always prioritized unity, trust, and loyalty, which have been instrumental in building a cohesive and resilient company culture. This commitment to family values has fostered a sense of belonging among employees and has contributed to their long-term dedication to the company.

4.1.3 Innovation and Product Excellence

Ferrero's success can also be attributed to its relentless pursuit of innovation and product

excellence. The company has consistently introduced new and exciting products that capture the imagination of consumers worldwide. From the unique combination of hazelnuts and chocolate in Nutella to the delicate layers of Ferrero Rocher, Ferrero has continuously pushed the boundaries of confectionery.

To ensure the highest quality standards, Ferrero has implemented rigorous quality control measures at every stage of the production process. The company sources the finest ingredients and employs state-of-the-art manufacturing techniques to deliver products that consistently exceed customer expectations. This unwavering commitment to excellence has earned Ferrero a reputation for producing some of the world's most beloved confections.

4.1.4 Balancing Tradition and Modernity

One of the remarkable aspects of Ferrero's success is its ability to balance tradition with modernity. While the company has embraced innovation and adapted to changing consumer preferences, it has also remained true to its roots. Ferrero continues to use traditional recipes and production methods, ensuring that the essence of their products remains unchanged.

The Ferrero family's commitment to preserving tradition extends beyond their products. They have also made significant efforts to support local communities and protect the environment. Ferrero has implemented sustainable sourcing practices, reducing its environmental impact and promoting the well-being of farmers and communities involved in the production of their ingredients.

4.1.5 Lessons from Ferrero's Success

Other companies can learn valuable lessons from Ferrero's success. Firstly, the importance of family values cannot be overstated. Building a strong company culture based on trust, loyalty, and unity can create a sense of purpose and commitment among employees, leading to long-term success.

Secondly, innovation and product excellence are crucial for staying ahead in a competitive market. Companies should continuously strive to develop new and exciting products that meet the evolving needs and preferences of consumers. By investing in research and development and maintaining stringent quality control measures, companies can establish themselves as leaders in their respective industries.

Lastly, finding the right balance between tradition and modernity is essential. While embracing innovation is necessary for growth, companies should also stay true to their roots and preserve the core values that define their brand. This balance can help companies maintain a sense of authenticity and build trust with their customers.

In conclusion, the Ferrero family's legacy is a testament to the power of family values, innovation, and a commitment to excellence. By embracing these principles, Ferrero has become a global leader in the confectionery industry. Other companies can learn from Ferrero's success by prioritizing family values, fostering innovation, and finding the right balance between tradition and modernity.

4.2 Ferrero's Product Innovation

Ferrero, the renowned Italian confectionery company, has become a household name with its iconic products such as Nutella, Ferrero Rocher, and Kinder Surprise. The success of Ferrero can be attributed to its relentless focus on product innovation, which has allowed the company to stay ahead of its competitors and maintain its position as a market leader.

4.2.1 A Legacy of Innovation

Ferrero's commitment to product innovation can be traced back to its founder, Pietro Ferrero. In the early 1940s, Pietro invented a new type of hazelnut and cocoa spread, which would later become the beloved Nutella. This innovative product not only revolutionized the breakfast table but also laid the foundation for Ferrero's future success.

Since then, Ferrero has continued to push the boundaries of confectionery innovation. The company invests heavily in research and development, constantly seeking new flavors, textures, and formats to captivate consumers' taste buds. Ferrero's dedication to innovation has resulted in a diverse range of products that cater to different consumer preferences and market segments.

4.2.2 Creating Unique Experiences

One of the key aspects of Ferrero's product innovation strategy is its focus on creating unique experiences for consumers. The company understands that it is not just about the taste of the product but also the overall experience that it offers. Ferrero achieves this by combining high-quality ingredients, exquisite packaging, and clever marketing campaigns.

For example, Ferrero Rocher, the famous chocolate hazelnut ball, is not just a delicious treat but also a symbol of luxury and indulgence. The gold foil wrapping, the delicate layers of chocolate and hazelnut, and the elegant packaging all contribute to the premium experience that consumers associate with Ferrero Rocher.

Similarly, Kinder Surprise, the chocolate egg with a surprise toy inside, offers a sense of excitement and anticipation for both children and adults. The element of surprise and the joy of discovering a new toy create a unique experience that sets Kinder Surprise apart from other confectionery products.

4.2.3 Balancing Tradition and Innovation

While Ferrero is known for its innovative products, the company also places great importance on preserving its traditions and heritage. Ferrero understands that its success is built on the trust and loyalty of its consumers, who have come to associate the brand with quality and authenticity.

To maintain this trust, Ferrero carefully balances tradition and innovation in its product development process. The company takes pride in using high-quality ingredients and traditional production methods, ensuring that its products meet the highest standards of taste and quality. At the same time,

Ferrero embraces new technologies and trends to create innovative products that cater to evolving consumer preferences.

This balance between tradition and innovation is exemplified in Ferrero's commitment to sustainable sourcing and production. The company actively works towards reducing its environmental impact and ensuring the long-term sustainability of its supply chain. By combining traditional values with modern practices, Ferrero demonstrates its dedication to both its consumers and the planet.

4.2.4 Lessons from Ferrero's Success

Other companies can learn valuable lessons from Ferrero's approach to product innovation:

1. Embrace continuous research and development: Investing in research and development is crucial for staying ahead of the competition and meeting changing consumer demands. Companies should allocate resources to explore new ideas, flavors, and formats to keep their product offerings fresh and exciting.

2. Create unique experiences: Beyond the product itself, companies should focus on creating memorable experiences for consumers. By paying attention to packaging, branding, and marketing, companies can differentiate themselves and build strong emotional connections with their customers.

3. Balance tradition and innovation: It is essential to strike a balance between

preserving traditions and embracing innovation. Companies should leverage their heritage and core values while adapting to new technologies and trends to meet the evolving needs of consumers.

4. Commit to sustainability: In today's environmentally conscious world, companies must prioritize sustainability in their product development and production processes. By adopting sustainable practices, companies can not only reduce their environmental impact but also enhance their brand reputation and appeal to socially conscious consumers.

Ferrero's success in product innovation is a testament to the power of combining creativity, quality, and consumer-centricity. By understanding the importance of creating unique experiences, balancing tradition and innovation, and embracing sustainability, companies can learn valuable lessons from Ferrero's journey and apply them to their own businesses.

4.3 Balancing Tradition and Modernity

In the ever-evolving business landscape, finding the right balance between tradition and modernity is crucial for the success and longevity of any company. This delicate equilibrium becomes even more challenging for family companies, as they navigate the complexities of generational transitions and changing market dynamics. In this section, we will explore how some of the most successful family companies, including Ferrero, Benetton, and Maina, have managed to strike this balance and what lessons other companies can learn from their experiences.

4.3.1 Embracing the Legacy

One of the key aspects of balancing tradition and modernity is acknowledging and embracing the legacy of the family company. Successful family companies understand the importance of their heritage and the values that have been passed down through generations. They recognize that their history and traditions are not obstacles to progress but rather a foundation upon which they can build for the future.

For example, Ferrero, the renowned Italian confectionery company, has managed to maintain its commitment to quality and innovation while staying true to its roots. The Ferrero family legacy, dating back to its founder, Pietro Ferrero, has instilled a sense of pride and responsibility in the company's current leaders. By honoring their heritage, Ferrero has been able to strike a balance between tradition and modernity, creating products that resonate with consumers while staying true to their core values.

4.3.2 Embracing Innovation

While tradition provides a strong foundation, successful family companies understand the need to embrace innovation and adapt to changing times. They recognize that staying stagnant is not an option in today's fast-paced business environment. By combining the wisdom of the past with the creativity of the present, these companies are able to stay relevant and competitive.

Benetton, the Italian fashion brand, is a prime example of a family company that has successfully embraced innovation. Known for its bold and colorful designs, Benetton has continuously pushed the boundaries of fashion while staying true to its core values of diversity and social impact. By embracing modern design techniques and technologies, Benetton has been able to maintain its relevance in an ever-changing industry.

4.3.3 Nurturing Entrepreneurial Spirit

Successful family companies understand the importance of nurturing an entrepreneurial spirit within their organizations. They encourage innovation and creativity while providing a supportive environment for new ideas to flourish. By empowering their employees and family members to take risks and explore new opportunities, these companies are able to adapt to changing market demands while preserving their core values.

Maina, a family-owned bakery known for its traditional baking techniques, has successfully balanced tradition and modernity by fostering an entrepreneurial spirit within the company. While staying true to their artisanal roots, Maina has embraced modern technology and processes to improve efficiency and expand their reach. By encouraging their employees to think outside the box and explore new avenues, Maina has been able to maintain its commitment to quality while adapting to the demands of a modern market.

4.3.4 Embracing Change and Continuous Learning

To balance tradition and modernity, successful family companies understand the importance of embracing change and continuously learning. They are not afraid to challenge the status quo and adapt their strategies to meet the evolving needs of their customers and the market. By staying open-minded and receptive to new ideas, these companies are able to stay ahead of the curve and remain competitive.

Kaiser, a family-owned food production company, exemplifies the importance of embracing change. Through continuous innovation in their production processes and product offerings, Kaiser has been able to expand its reach and establish itself as a leader in the food industry. By staying agile and adaptable, Kaiser has successfully balanced tradition and modernity, ensuring the company's continued growth and success.

4.3.5 Building a Strong Corporate Culture

A strong corporate culture is essential for balancing tradition and modernity in family companies. Successful companies understand the importance of fostering a culture that values both the wisdom of the past and the innovation of the present. By creating an environment that encourages collaboration, open communication, and a shared sense of purpose, these companies are able to navigate the challenges of generational transitions and adapt to changing market dynamics.

Esselunga, a family-owned retail company, has built a strong corporate culture that embraces both tradition and modernity. By fostering a customer-

centric approach and empowering their employees to take ownership of their roles, Esselunga has been able to stay ahead of the competition in the retail industry. By nurturing a culture of continuous improvement and innovation, Esselunga has successfully balanced tradition and modernity, ensuring the company's long-term success.

4.3.6 Lessons for Other Companies

The success stories of family companies like Ferrero, Benetton, Maina, and Esselunga offer valuable lessons for other companies looking to balance tradition and modernity. These lessons include:

1. Embrace your heritage: Acknowledge and honor your company's history and values while adapting to the changing times.

2. Foster innovation: Encourage creativity and embrace new ideas to stay relevant and competitive in a rapidly evolving business landscape.

3. Nurture an entrepreneurial spirit: Empower your employees to take risks and explore new opportunities, fostering a culture of innovation and growth.

4. Embrace change and continuous learning: Stay open-minded and adaptable, embracing change and continuously learning to meet the evolving needs of your customers and the market.

5. Build a strong corporate culture: Foster a culture that values both tradition and

modernity, encouraging collaboration, open communication, and a shared sense of purpose.

By incorporating these lessons into their strategies, companies of all sizes and sectors can find the right balance between tradition and modernity, ensuring their long-term success and sustainability in an ever-changing business landscape.

4.4 Lessons from Ferrero's Success

Ferrero, a renowned Italian confectionery company, has achieved remarkable success over the years. The company's ability to balance tradition and innovation, along with its commitment to quality and product excellence, has made it a global leader in the chocolate and confectionery industry. Ferrero's success story offers valuable lessons for other companies looking to thrive in today's competitive business landscape.

4.4.1 Embrace a Strong Family Legacy

One of the key factors behind Ferrero's success is its strong family legacy. The company was founded by Pietro Ferrero in 1946 and is now led by his son, Giovanni Ferrero. Ferrero's commitment to preserving its family values and traditions has played a significant role in shaping its corporate culture and long-term vision. Other companies can learn from Ferrero's example by embracing their own unique family legacies and leveraging them as a source of strength and inspiration.

4.4.2 Foster a Culture of Product Innovation

Ferrero has consistently demonstrated its ability to innovate and create new products that capture the hearts of consumers worldwide. The company's commitment to product excellence and continuous innovation has allowed it to stay ahead of the competition. Ferrero's success in launching iconic products such as Nutella, Kinder Surprise, and Ferrero Rocher showcases the importance of fostering a culture of innovation within an organization. By encouraging creativity and providing resources for research and development, companies can unlock new opportunities for growth and success.

4.4.3 Balance Tradition and Modernity

Ferrero has successfully managed to balance its rich tradition with modernity, adapting to changing consumer preferences and market dynamics. While the company remains committed to its core values and traditional recipes, it has also embraced new technologies and manufacturing processes to enhance efficiency and meet evolving consumer demands. This ability to strike a balance between tradition and modernity has allowed Ferrero to maintain its brand identity while staying relevant in a rapidly changing world. Other companies can learn from Ferrero's approach by embracing innovation without compromising their core values and heritage.

4.4.4 Prioritize Quality and Excellence

Ferrero's unwavering commitment to quality and excellence has been a cornerstone of its success. The company places great emphasis on sourcing the finest ingredients, implementing rigorous quality control measures, and ensuring that every product meets the highest standards. This dedication to quality has earned Ferrero a reputation for excellence and has helped build trust and loyalty among its customers. Other companies can learn from Ferrero's focus on quality by prioritizing excellence in every aspect of their operations, from product development to customer service.

4.4.5 Cultivate Strong Family Values

Family values are deeply ingrained in Ferrero's corporate culture. The company places a strong emphasis on trust, respect, and collaboration, creating a supportive and inclusive work environment. Ferrero's commitment to its employees' well-being and professional growth has fostered a sense of loyalty and dedication among its workforce. By cultivating strong family values, companies can create a positive and nurturing workplace culture that attracts and retains top talent.

4.4.6 Build Strong Relationships with Suppliers and Partners

Ferrero's success is not solely attributed to its internal operations but also to its strong relationships with suppliers and partners. The company works closely with its suppliers to ensure the highest quality ingredients and maintains long-term partnerships with key stakeholders. This collaborative approach has enabled Ferrero to build a robust and reliable supply chain, ensuring the consistent delivery of high-quality products to its customers. Other companies can learn from Ferrero's emphasis on building strong relationships with suppliers and partners, as these alliances can contribute to overall business success.

4.4.7 Focus on Sustainability and Corporate Social Responsibility

Ferrero has made significant strides in integrating sustainability and corporate social responsibility into its business practices. The company is committed to sourcing sustainable ingredients, reducing its environmental impact, and supporting local communities. Ferrero's dedication to sustainability not only aligns with the values of today's socially conscious consumers but also contributes to long-term business success. By prioritizing sustainability and corporate social responsibility, companies can enhance their brand reputation, attract environmentally conscious consumers, and contribute to a more sustainable future.

4.4.8 Adapt to Changing Market Trends

Ferrero's ability to adapt to changing market trends has been instrumental in its success. The company has expanded its product portfolio to cater to evolving consumer preferences, including the introduction of healthier options and the expansion into new markets. Ferrero's agility and willingness to embrace change have allowed it to stay ahead of the curve and remain competitive in a dynamic business landscape. Other companies can learn from Ferrero's adaptability by continuously monitoring market trends, embracing innovation, and being open to new opportunities.

In conclusion, Ferrero's success can be attributed to a combination of factors, including embracing a strong family legacy, fostering a culture of innovation, balancing tradition and modernity, prioritizing quality and excellence, cultivating strong family values, building strong relationships with suppliers and partners, focusing on sustainability and corporate social responsibility, and adapting to changing market trends. By incorporating these lessons into their own strategies, companies from various sectors and sizes can increase their chances of achieving long-term success and sustainability.

Patagonia

5.1 The Patagonia Story

Patagonia is a renowned outdoor clothing and gear company that has gained recognition not only for its high-quality products but also for its commitment to environmental sustainability and ethical business practices. Founded in 1973 by Yvon Chouinard, Patagonia has become a global leader in the outdoor industry, inspiring other companies to prioritize sustainability and social responsibility.

5.1.1 The Early Years and Founding Principles

The story of Patagonia begins with Yvon Chouinard's passion for climbing and his desire to create high-quality climbing equipment. In the early years, Chouinard Equipment, as it was initially known, focused on producing innovative climbing gear that met the needs of outdoor enthusiasts. However, as the company grew, Chouinard became increasingly aware of the negative impact that the manufacturing process had on the environment.

Chouinard's commitment to environmental responsibility led him to make significant changes in the way Patagonia operated. In 1991, the company made a bold move by pledging 1% of its sales to environmental causes. This commitment, known as the "1% for the Planet" initiative, has since inspired numerous companies to follow suit and contribute to environmental conservation efforts.

5.1.2 Environmental Sustainability as a Core Value

One of the key aspects that sets Patagonia apart from other companies is its unwavering commitment to environmental sustainability. The company has taken numerous steps to reduce its ecological footprint and promote sustainable practices throughout its supply chain.

Patagonia has implemented various initiatives to minimize waste, conserve energy, and reduce greenhouse gas emissions. For example, the company has invested in renewable energy sources, such as solar panels, to power its facilities. Additionally, Patagonia has implemented recycling programs and encourages customers to repair their products rather than replacing them, reducing the amount of waste that ends up in landfills.

Furthermore, Patagonia has been a vocal advocate for environmental causes, using its platform to raise awareness about pressing issues such as climate change and deforestation. The company has supported grassroots environmental organizations and has actively engaged in political advocacy to promote sustainable policies.

5.1.3 Ethical Leadership and Social Responsibility

In addition to its commitment to environmental sustainability, Patagonia has also demonstrated ethical leadership and social responsibility in its business practices. The company has prioritized fair labor practices and has taken steps to ensure that its supply chain is free from exploitation.

Patagonia has implemented strict labor standards and regularly audits its suppliers to ensure compliance with these standards. The company has also been transparent about its supply chain, providing customers with information about the factories and farms where its products are made.

Furthermore, Patagonia has been a pioneer in promoting work-life balance and employee well-being. The company offers flexible work schedules, encourages employees to pursue outdoor activities, and provides on-site childcare facilities. These initiatives have not only contributed to a positive work culture but have also attracted and retained top talent.

5.1.4 Lessons for Other Companies

The success of Patagonia can serve as a valuable lesson for other companies, regardless of their sector or size. Here are some key takeaways:

1. **Commitment to sustainability**: Patagonia's dedication to environmental sustainability has not only resonated with customers but has also helped the company differentiate itself in a crowded market. By prioritizing sustainability, companies can attract environmentally conscious consumers and contribute to a more sustainable future.

2. **Transparency and accountability**: Patagonia's transparency about its supply chain and labor practices has built trust with customers. Companies should strive for transparency and accountability in their operations, ensuring that they uphold ethical

standards and treat their employees and suppliers fairly.

3. **Social and environmental activism**: Patagonia's active engagement in environmental and social causes has helped the company build a strong brand identity and connect with like-minded customers. Companies can leverage their influence to advocate for positive change and align their values with those of their target audience.

4. **Long-term thinking**: Patagonia's focus on creating durable, high-quality products that stand the test of time aligns with a more sustainable and responsible approach to consumption. Companies should prioritize longevity and durability over planned obsolescence, reducing waste and promoting a circular economy.

5. **Employee well-being**: Patagonia's emphasis on work-life balance and employee well-being has contributed to a positive work culture and employee satisfaction. Companies should prioritize the well-being of their employees, fostering a healthy and supportive work environment.

In conclusion, Patagonia's success can be attributed to its unwavering commitment to environmental sustainability, ethical leadership, and social responsibility. By prioritizing these values, companies can not only achieve financial success but also make a positive impact on the planet and society as a whole.

5.2 Patagonia's Commitment to Sustainability

Patagonia, an outdoor clothing and gear company, has become a shining example of how a family company can prioritize sustainability and environmental responsibility while still achieving remarkable success. Founded by Yvon Chouinard in 1973, Patagonia has grown into a global brand known for its high-quality products and unwavering commitment to protecting the planet.

5.2.1 A Vision for a Sustainable Future

From its inception, Patagonia has been driven by a strong environmental ethos. Yvon Chouinard, an avid climber and outdoorsman, recognized the need to preserve the natural world that served as the backdrop for his adventures. This vision for a sustainable future has guided the company's decision-making process and shaped its core values.

Patagonia's commitment to sustainability is evident in its mission statement, which reads, "Build the best product, cause no unnecessary harm, use business to inspire and implement solutions to the environmental crisis." This mission statement serves as a guiding principle for the company, influencing everything from product design to supply chain management.

5.2.2 Environmental Stewardship in Action

Patagonia's commitment to sustainability goes beyond mere rhetoric. The company has implemented numerous initiatives to reduce its environmental impact and promote responsible business practices. One of the most notable initiatives is the "Worn Wear" program, which encourages customers to repair and reuse their Patagonia products rather than buying new ones. This program not only extends the lifespan of the products but also reduces the demand for new resources and minimizes waste.

Additionally, Patagonia has taken significant steps to address the environmental impact of its supply chain. The company is a pioneer in using recycled materials in its products, such as recycled polyester made from plastic bottles. Patagonia also prioritizes fair labor practices and partners with suppliers who share its commitment to social and environmental responsibility.

5.2.3 Transparency and Accountability

Patagonia understands the importance of transparency and accountability in building trust with its customers. The company openly shares information about its environmental initiatives, including its carbon footprint, water usage, and waste management practices. By being transparent about its impact, Patagonia holds itself accountable and encourages other companies to do the same.

Furthermore, Patagonia actively engages with its customers and the wider community to raise awareness about environmental issues. The company uses its platform to advocate for policies that protect the planet and supports grassroots environmental organizations through its "1% for the Planet" program, where it donates 1% of its sales to environmental causes.

5.2.4 Family Values Driving Sustainability

One of the key factors that sets Patagonia apart is its family-oriented approach to business. As a family company, Patagonia has the advantage of being able to make long-term decisions that prioritize sustainability over short-term profits. The Chouinard family, led by Yvon Chouinard and his children, has instilled a deep sense of responsibility for the environment in the company's culture.

The Chouinard family's commitment to sustainability is not just limited to the company's operations but extends to their personal lives as well. They lead by example, actively participating in environmental initiatives and living a sustainable lifestyle. This alignment between their personal values and the company's mission creates a strong sense of purpose and unity within Patagonia.

5.2.5 Lessons for Other Companies

Patagonia's success and commitment to sustainability offer valuable lessons for other companies looking to incorporate environmental responsibility into their business practices:

1. **Align values with actions**: Patagonia's success stems from its ability to align its core values with its actions. By integrating sustainability into every aspect of the business, companies can create a cohesive and authentic brand identity.

2. **Transparency and accountability**: Being transparent about environmental impact and holding oneself accountable fosters trust with

customers and stakeholders. Companies should strive to share information openly and actively engage with their communities.

3. **Long-term thinking**: Family companies have the advantage of making decisions with a long-term perspective. By prioritizing sustainability over short-term gains, companies can build a resilient and future-proof business.

4. **Collaboration and advocacy**: Patagonia's commitment to environmental causes extends beyond its own operations. Companies can make a significant impact by collaborating with like-minded organizations and advocating for policies that promote sustainability.

5. **Innovation and adaptation**: Patagonia's success is rooted in its ability to innovate and adapt to changing market demands. Companies should continuously seek new ways to reduce their environmental footprint and embrace sustainable practices.

In conclusion, Patagonia's commitment to sustainability serves as an inspiration for companies across industries. By integrating environmental responsibility into their business practices, companies can not only contribute to a more sustainable future but also build a strong and resilient brand that resonates with customers who prioritize ethical and environmentally conscious choices.

5.3 Family Values in Patagonia's Business Practices

Patagonia, a renowned outdoor clothing and gear company, has gained recognition not only for its high-quality products but also for its commitment to environmental responsibility and ethical leadership. The company's success can be attributed, in large part, to the strong influence of family values in its business practices. Patagonia's unique approach to incorporating these values has set it apart from other companies and serves as a valuable lesson for businesses across industries.

5.3.1 A Culture of Environmental Stewardship

At the core of Patagonia's business practices is a deep-rooted commitment to environmental stewardship. This commitment stems from the personal values of the company's founder, Yvon Chouinard, and has been ingrained in the company's culture from its inception. Patagonia's dedication to protecting the environment is not merely a marketing strategy but a genuine belief that business can and should be a force for positive change.

5.3.2 Transparency and Accountability

One of the key aspects of Patagonia's family values is its emphasis on transparency and accountability. The company believes in being open and honest with its customers, employees, and stakeholders. Patagonia actively communicates its environmental initiatives, challenges, and progress, allowing others to hold them accountable. This level of transparency builds trust and fosters a sense of shared responsibility among all stakeholders.

5.3.3 Work-Life Balance and Employee Well-being

Patagonia recognizes the importance of work-life balance and the well-being of its employees. The company understands that happy and fulfilled employees are more productive and engaged. Patagonia offers flexible work arrangements, encourages employees to pursue their passions outside of work, and provides numerous benefits such as on-site childcare, paid parental leave, and wellness programs. By prioritizing the well-being of its employees, Patagonia creates a positive and supportive work environment.

5.3.4 Long-Term Thinking and Sustainable Growth

Family values play a crucial role in Patagonia's long-term thinking and commitment to sustainable growth. The company focuses on creating products that are built to last, reducing waste, and minimizing its environmental footprint. Patagonia actively encourages its customers to repair and reuse their products rather than buying new ones, promoting a culture of sustainability and responsible consumption. By prioritizing long-term sustainability over short-term profits, Patagonia has built a loyal customer base and a strong brand reputation.

5.3.5 Giving Back to the Community

Patagonia's family values extend beyond its own operations and into the communities it serves. The company actively supports grassroots environmental organizations through its "1% for the Planet" initiative, where it donates 1% of its sales to environmental causes. Patagonia also encourages its employees to volunteer and engage in community service. By giving back to the community, Patagonia demonstrates its commitment to making a positive impact beyond its bottom line.

5.3.6 Ethical Supply Chain Practices

Patagonia's family values are reflected in its ethical supply chain practices. The company takes great care in sourcing materials and manufacturing its products in a socially and environmentally responsible manner. Patagonia works closely with its suppliers to ensure fair labor practices, safe working conditions, and the use of sustainable materials. By holding itself and its suppliers to high ethical standards, Patagonia sets an example for other companies to follow.

5.3.7 Authentic Brand Storytelling

Patagonia's family values are effectively communicated through its authentic brand storytelling. The company shares stories of its environmental initiatives, the people behind its products, and the impact it is making in the world. Patagonia's brand messaging is consistent, genuine, and resonates with its target audience. By sharing its values and mission through storytelling, Patagonia creates a strong emotional connection with its customers and builds brand loyalty.

5.3.8 Collaboration and Partnerships

Patagonia understands the power of collaboration and partnerships in driving positive change. The company actively seeks out like-minded organizations and individuals to work together on environmental initiatives. Patagonia believes that by joining forces with others who share its values, it can have a greater impact and create lasting change. This collaborative approach sets an example for other companies to collaborate for the greater good.

In conclusion, Patagonia's success can be attributed to its strong adherence to family values in its business practices. The company's commitment to environmental stewardship, transparency, employee well-being, long-term thinking, community engagement, ethical supply chain practices, authentic brand storytelling, and collaboration serve as valuable lessons for other companies. By incorporating these values into their own operations, businesses can create a positive impact on society, build strong relationships with stakeholders, and achieve long-term success.

5.4 Applying Patagonia's Ethical Leadership to Other Companies

Patagonia is widely recognized as a leader in ethical business practices and environmental responsibility. The company's commitment to sustainability and its unique approach to leadership have set it apart from other companies in various industries. By examining Patagonia's ethical leadership, other companies can gain valuable insights and learn how to incorporate similar practices into their own operations.

One of the key aspects of Patagonia's ethical leadership is its unwavering commitment to environmental responsibility. The company has consistently demonstrated its dedication to minimizing its ecological footprint and promoting sustainable practices. Other companies can learn from Patagonia's approach by prioritizing environmental sustainability in their own operations.

To apply Patagonia's ethical leadership, companies can start by conducting a thorough assessment of their environmental impact. This includes evaluating their supply chain, production processes, and waste management systems. By identifying areas where improvements can be made, companies can implement sustainable practices that align with their values and contribute to a healthier planet.

Furthermore, companies can follow Patagonia's lead by actively engaging in environmental advocacy. By using their platform to raise awareness about pressing environmental issues, companies can inspire change and encourage others to adopt sustainable practices. This not only benefits the environment but also enhances a company's reputation and strengthens its relationship with customers who value sustainability.

5.4.2 Prioritizing Ethical Supply Chains

Patagonia has been a pioneer in promoting ethical supply chains. The company places a strong emphasis on ensuring that its products are sourced and manufactured in a socially responsible manner.

By prioritizing fair labor practices and transparency, Patagonia has set a high standard for other companies to follow.

To apply Patagonia's ethical leadership, companies should start by thoroughly examining their supply chains. This involves conducting audits and assessments to identify any potential ethical issues, such as labor exploitation or environmental harm. By working closely with suppliers and holding them accountable to high ethical standards, companies can ensure that their products are produced in a responsible and sustainable manner.

Additionally, companies can learn from Patagonia's approach by actively supporting fair trade and responsible sourcing initiatives. By partnering with organizations that promote ethical practices, companies can contribute to the overall improvement of supply chain standards across industries. This not only benefits workers and communities but also enhances a company's reputation and builds trust with consumers.

5.4.3 Fostering a Culture of Transparency and Accountability

Patagonia's ethical leadership is deeply rooted in its commitment to transparency and accountability. The company has been open about its successes and failures, and it actively encourages its employees and customers to hold it accountable. This culture of transparency has helped Patagonia build trust and establish itself as a leader in ethical business practices.

To apply Patagonia's ethical leadership, companies should prioritize transparency in their operations. This includes openly sharing information about their environmental and social impact, as well as their efforts to improve. By being transparent, companies can build trust with their stakeholders and demonstrate their commitment to ethical practices.

Furthermore, companies can foster a culture of accountability by actively seeking feedback from employees, customers, and other stakeholders. By listening to their concerns and addressing them in a timely and transparent manner, companies can show that they value the opinions and well-being of those they interact with. This not only helps companies identify areas for improvement but also strengthens their relationships with stakeholders.

5.4.4 Investing in Employee Well-being and Development

Patagonia's ethical leadership extends to its approach to employee well-being and development. The company recognizes the importance of creating a positive work environment and investing in the growth and development of its employees. Other companies can learn from Patagonia's approach by prioritizing the well-being and professional development of their own employees.

To apply Patagonia's ethical leadership, companies should focus on creating a supportive and inclusive work culture. This includes providing employees with opportunities for growth, fostering work-life balance, and promoting diversity and inclusion. By investing in their employees' well-being, companies can enhance employee satisfaction and productivity, leading to long-term success.

Additionally, companies can learn from Patagonia's approach to employee development by providing ongoing training and learning opportunities. By empowering employees with the skills and knowledge they need to succeed, companies can foster a culture of continuous improvement and innovation.

Conclusion

Patagonia's ethical leadership serves as a powerful example for other companies looking to incorporate sustainable and ethical practices into their operations. By emphasizing environmental responsibility, prioritizing ethical supply chains, fostering transparency and accountability, and investing in employee well-being and development, companies can learn from Patagonia's success and make a positive impact in their respective industries. By applying these principles, companies can not only contribute to a more sustainable and ethical business landscape but also enhance their own long-term success and reputation.

Volkswagen

6.1 The Volkswagen Family Legacy

The Volkswagen Group, one of the world's largest automotive manufacturers, has a rich family legacy that has played a significant role in shaping the company's history and success. Founded in 1937 by the German Labour Front, Volkswagen has evolved into a global powerhouse under the leadership of the Porsche and Piëch families. This section will explore the Volkswagen family legacy and its impact on the company's growth, as well as the lessons that other companies can learn from their experiences.

6.1.1 The Origins of Volkswagen

The Volkswagen story began with the vision of Adolf Hitler, who aimed to create an affordable and reliable car for the German people. The company's first model, the iconic Volkswagen Beetle, quickly gained popularity and became a symbol of German engineering excellence. However, it was not until after World War II that the Porsche and Piëch families became involved in the company.

6.1.2 Family Involvement and Leadership

The Porsche and Piëch families have played a crucial role in the success of Volkswagen. Ferdinand Porsche, the founder of the Porsche brand, was instrumental in the development of the original Volkswagen Beetle. His grandson, Ferdinand Piëch, later became the CEO of Volkswagen and transformed the company into a global automotive giant.

The family's commitment to the company's success is evident in their long-term involvement and dedication. The Porsche and Piëch families have maintained significant ownership stakes in Volkswagen, ensuring their continued influence and commitment to the company's growth.

6.1.3 Overcoming Scandals and Rebuilding Trust

In recent years, Volkswagen faced significant challenges due to the "dieselgate" scandal, where the company was found to have manipulated emissions tests. This scandal severely damaged Volkswagen's reputation and led to substantial financial and legal consequences. However, the family's commitment to the company's values and long-term vision played a crucial role in navigating this crisis.

The Volkswagen family legacy provided a foundation of trust and integrity that helped the company weather the storm. The family took swift action to address the issue, holding individuals accountable and implementing measures to prevent similar incidents in the future. Their hands-on approach and commitment to transparency were essential in rebuilding trust with customers, stakeholders, and the public.

6.1.4 Family Governance and Values

Family governance has been a key aspect of the Volkswagen family legacy. The Porsche and Piëch families have established a strong governance structure that ensures the long-term stability and success of the company. This structure includes family councils, supervisory boards, and clear guidelines for family involvement in the business.

The family's values, such as integrity, innovation, and sustainability, have also played a significant role in shaping Volkswagen's corporate culture. These values are deeply ingrained in the company's operations and guide decision-making at all levels. The family's commitment to these values has helped Volkswagen maintain a strong sense of purpose and direction, even during challenging times.

6.1.5 Lessons in Crisis Management

The Volkswagen family legacy offers valuable lessons in crisis management for other companies facing similar challenges. Firstly, maintaining a strong commitment to core values and ethics is crucial in navigating crises and rebuilding trust. Volkswagen's swift action and transparency in addressing the dieselgate scandal demonstrated their dedication to upholding their values.

Secondly, family involvement and long-term vision can provide stability and resilience during times of crisis. The Porsche and Piëch families' continued commitment to the company's success helped Volkswagen weather the storm and emerge stronger.

Lastly, effective family governance structures are essential for maintaining stability and ensuring the long-term success of a family business. Clear guidelines for family involvement, combined with professional management practices, can help strike a balance between family influence and professional decision-making.

6.1.6 Conclusion

The Volkswagen family legacy is a testament to the power of family involvement and values in driving the success of a company. The Porsche and Piëch families' commitment to the company's long-term vision, combined with their strong governance structure, has helped Volkswagen overcome challenges and maintain its position as a global leader in the automotive industry.

Other companies can learn from Volkswagen's experiences by prioritizing their core values, establishing effective governance structures, and fostering a long-term vision. By doing so, companies can navigate crises, rebuild trust, and ensure sustainable growth for future generations. The Volkswagen family legacy serves as an inspiration for businesses across industries to harness the power of family values and involvement in achieving long-term success.

6.2 Overcoming Scandals and Rebuilding Trust

In the world of business, scandals can have a devastating impact on a company's reputation and trustworthiness. Family companies, just like any other, are not immune to such challenges. However, what sets successful family companies apart is their ability to overcome these scandals and rebuild trust with their stakeholders. In this section, we will explore how some of the most successful family companies, including Volkswagen, have navigated through scandals and regained the trust of their customers, employees, and the public.

6.2.1 The Volkswagen Emissions Scandal

One of the most prominent scandals in recent years was the Volkswagen emissions scandal, also known as "Dieselgate." In 2015, it was revealed that Volkswagen had installed software in their diesel vehicles to manipulate emissions tests, leading to significantly higher pollution levels than reported. This revelation not only tarnished Volkswagen's reputation but also raised questions about the integrity of the entire automotive industry.

6.2.2 Taking Responsibility and Accountability

When faced with a scandal of such magnitude, the first step for any company is to take responsibility for their actions. Volkswagen acknowledged the wrongdoing and publicly apologized for betraying the trust of their customers, regulators, and the public. The company's top executives, including members of the Volkswagen family, expressed their remorse and commitment to rectifying the situation.

6.2.3 Implementing Structural Changes

To rebuild trust, Volkswagen recognized the need for significant structural changes within the company. They appointed new leadership, including a new CEO, who was tasked with implementing a cultural shift towards transparency and ethical behavior. The company also established an independent compliance committee to ensure adherence to regulations and ethical standards.

6.2.4 Strengthening Governance and Compliance

Family governance played a crucial role in Volkswagen's recovery process. The company strengthened its governance structures by separating the roles of the CEO and the Chairman of the Board, ensuring a more independent oversight of the company's operations. Additionally, Volkswagen implemented stricter compliance measures and internal controls to prevent similar incidents in the future.

6.2.5 Investing in Electric Vehicles and Sustainability

To regain trust and demonstrate their commitment to environmental responsibility, Volkswagen made significant investments in electric vehicles (EVs) and sustainable mobility solutions. The company pledged to transition to a more sustainable future by investing billions of dollars in EV technology and infrastructure. This strategic shift not only helped rebuild trust but also positioned Volkswagen as a leader in the emerging EV market.

6.2.6 Rebuilding Customer Confidence

Rebuilding trust with customers was a top priority for Volkswagen. The company launched various initiatives to regain customer confidence, including extended warranties, free maintenance programs, and enhanced customer service. Volkswagen also implemented rigorous quality control measures to ensure the safety and reliability of their vehicles.

6.2.7 Transparency and Communication

Open and transparent communication is vital during times of crisis. Volkswagen recognized the importance of rebuilding trust through effective communication. The company provided regular updates on their progress in addressing the scandal, including the implementation of new compliance measures and the development of sustainable mobility solutions. By being transparent about their actions and progress, Volkswagen aimed to regain the trust of their stakeholders.

6.2.8 Learning from Mistakes

The Volkswagen scandal served as a wake-up call not only for the company but also for the entire automotive industry. It highlighted the importance of ethical behavior, transparency, and environmental responsibility. Volkswagen's experience serves as a valuable lesson for other companies, emphasizing the need for strong governance, compliance, and a commitment to sustainability.

6.2.9 Rebuilding Trust Takes Time

Rebuilding trust is a long and challenging process. It requires consistent actions, transparency, and a genuine commitment to change. Volkswagen understood that regaining trust would not happen overnight and that it would require sustained efforts over an extended period. By staying true to their commitments and consistently delivering on their promises, Volkswagen gradually rebuilt trust with their stakeholders.

6.2.10 Lessons for Other Companies

The Volkswagen scandal provides valuable lessons for other companies facing similar challenges. It underscores the importance of taking responsibility, implementing structural changes, strengthening governance and compliance, investing in sustainability, rebuilding customer confidence, transparent communication, learning from mistakes, and recognizing that rebuilding trust takes time.

By studying the experiences of successful family companies like Volkswagen, other organizations can learn how to navigate through scandals, rebuild trust, and emerge stronger. The key lies in embracing transparency, accountability, and a genuine commitment to change, while staying true to the core values and principles that define the company's identity.

6.3 Family Governance in Volkswagen

Family governance plays a crucial role in the success and longevity of family-owned companies. It involves establishing structures, processes, and policies that ensure effective decision-making, succession planning, and the preservation of family values. Volkswagen, one of the world's largest automobile manufacturers, is a prime example of a family company that has implemented strong family governance practices.

6.3.1 The Volkswagen Family Legacy

Volkswagen has a rich family legacy that dates back to its founding in 1937. The company was established by the German Labour Front and was

later privatized, with the Porsche and Piëch families becoming major shareholders. The Porsche and Piëch families have played a significant role in shaping the company's direction and success over the years.

6.3.2 Family Involvement in Decision-Making

One of the key aspects of family governance in Volkswagen is the active involvement of family members in decision-making processes. The Porsche and Piëch families have representation on the company's supervisory board, which allows them to have a say in major strategic decisions. This ensures that the family's long-term vision and values are taken into account when shaping the company's direction.

6.3.3 Balancing Family and Business Interests

A critical challenge for family-owned companies is finding the right balance between family interests and the needs of the business. In Volkswagen, family governance mechanisms are in place to address this challenge. The supervisory board consists of both family members and independent directors, ensuring a diversity of perspectives and expertise. This helps prevent conflicts of interest and ensures that decisions are made in the best interest of the company.

6.3.4 Succession Planning and Leadership Development

Successful family companies understand the importance of effective succession planning and leadership development. Volkswagen has

implemented robust processes to identify and groom the next generation of leaders within the family. This ensures a smooth transition of leadership and continuity in the company's strategic direction. By investing in leadership development programs and providing opportunities for family members to gain experience in different areas of the business, Volkswagen prepares the next generation to take on key roles within the company.

6.3.5 Preserving Family Values

Family values are often at the core of family-owned companies, and preserving these values is crucial for their long-term success. In Volkswagen, family governance mechanisms are designed to ensure that the company's operations align with the family's values. This includes promoting sustainability, ethical business practices, and social responsibility. By upholding these values, Volkswagen not only maintains its reputation but also attracts customers and stakeholders who share similar values.

6.3.6 Communication and Transparency

Open communication and transparency are essential in family-owned companies to build trust and maintain strong relationships between family members and non-family employees. In Volkswagen, family governance practices emphasize the importance of clear and open communication channels. Regular family meetings, where family members can discuss both family and business matters, help foster a sense of unity and shared purpose. Additionally, transparent reporting and disclosure practices ensure that all stakeholders are well-informed about the company's performance and decision-making processes.

6.3.7 Long-Term Perspective

Family-owned companies often have a long-term perspective, focusing on sustainable growth and preserving the company for future generations. In Volkswagen, family governance practices encourage a strategic outlook that goes beyond short-term financial gains. This long-term perspective allows the company to make decisions that prioritize the company's longevity and reputation, rather than solely focusing on immediate profits.

6.3.8 Lessons for Other Companies

Other companies can learn valuable lessons from Volkswagen's family governance practices. Firstly, involving family members in decision-making processes can bring a unique perspective and ensure the preservation of family values. However, it is crucial to strike a balance between family interests and the needs of the business by including independent directors and implementing robust governance mechanisms.

Secondly, effective succession planning and leadership development are vital for the continuity and success of family-owned companies. By investing in the development of the next generation of leaders, companies can ensure a smooth transition and maintain their strategic direction.

Lastly, upholding family values and promoting transparency and communication are essential for building trust and maintaining strong relationships

within the company and with external stakeholders. By aligning business operations with family values and fostering open communication, companies can create a positive corporate culture and attract like-minded employees and customers.

In conclusion, family governance is a critical factor in the success of family-owned companies like Volkswagen. By implementing effective governance structures, involving family members in decision-making, and preserving family values, Volkswagen has been able to navigate challenges and maintain its position as a global leader in the automobile industry. Other companies can learn from Volkswagen's family governance practices and adapt them to their own contexts to drive long-term success and sustainability.

6.4 Lessons in Crisis Management from Volkswagen

Crisis management is an essential skill for any company, regardless of its size or industry. It is during times of crisis that a company's true character and leadership are put to the test. One company that has faced significant challenges in recent years is Volkswagen. The German automotive giant, known for its iconic Beetle and innovative engineering, found itself at the center of a major scandal in 2015. The company was accused of cheating on emissions tests, which resulted in a significant loss of trust and reputation. However, Volkswagen's response to the crisis provides valuable lessons for other companies facing similar challenges.

6.4.1 Transparency and Accountability

One of the key lessons from Volkswagen's crisis management is the importance of transparency and accountability. When the scandal broke, Volkswagen initially denied any wrongdoing. However, as evidence mounted, the company had to acknowledge its mistakes and take responsibility for its actions. This level of transparency and accountability is crucial in rebuilding trust with stakeholders, including customers, employees, and investors. By admitting fault and taking immediate action to rectify the situation, Volkswagen demonstrated a commitment to transparency and accountability.

6.4.2 Effective Communication

During a crisis, effective communication is vital to manage the situation and maintain trust. Volkswagen recognized the importance of clear and consistent messaging throughout the crisis. The company's CEO, Matthias Müller, publicly apologized for the emissions scandal and outlined the steps the company would take to address the issue. Volkswagen also established a dedicated website to provide regular updates on the progress of investigations and the implementation of corrective measures. By communicating openly and honestly, Volkswagen aimed to regain the trust of its stakeholders and demonstrate its commitment to resolving the crisis.

6.4.3 Swift Action and Remediation

In times of crisis, swift action is crucial to mitigate the damage and restore confidence. Volkswagen took

immediate steps to address the emissions scandal by recalling affected vehicles, implementing stricter emissions testing procedures, and investing in electric vehicle technology. The company also appointed a new CEO, Herbert Diess, who spearheaded efforts to transform Volkswagen's corporate culture and prioritize sustainability. By taking decisive action and demonstrating a commitment to rectifying the issue, Volkswagen showed its determination to learn from its mistakes and rebuild its reputation.

6.4.4 Learning from Mistakes

One of the most significant lessons from Volkswagen's crisis management is the importance of learning from mistakes. The emissions scandal served as a wake-up call for the company, highlighting the need for stronger ethical practices and a more sustainable approach to business. Volkswagen embarked on a journey of introspection and transformation, reevaluating its corporate values and implementing measures to prevent similar incidents in the future. By acknowledging its mistakes and actively seeking to learn from them, Volkswagen demonstrated a commitment to continuous improvement and ethical conduct.

6.4.5 Strengthening Corporate Governance

Another crucial lesson from Volkswagen's crisis management is the importance of strengthening corporate governance. The scandal exposed weaknesses in the company's governance structure, allowing unethical behavior to go undetected. In response, Volkswagen implemented significant changes to its governance practices, including the establishment of an independent compliance committee and the appointment of external auditors to monitor compliance with ethical standards. By enhancing its corporate governance, Volkswagen aimed to prevent future misconduct and ensure greater transparency and accountability within the organization.

6.4.6 Rebuilding Trust and Reputation

Rebuilding trust and reputation is a long and challenging process, particularly after a significant crisis. Volkswagen recognized the importance of this task and implemented various initiatives to regain the trust of its stakeholders. The company launched a comprehensive marketing campaign to emphasize its commitment to sustainability and electric mobility. Volkswagen also invested heavily in research and development to develop innovative and environmentally friendly vehicles. By demonstrating a genuine commitment to change and sustainability, Volkswagen aimed to rebuild its reputation and regain the trust of its customers and the public.

6.4.7 Collaboration and Partnerships

Lastly, Volkswagen's crisis management highlighted the importance of collaboration and partnerships. The company recognized that addressing the emissions scandal required the collective efforts of various stakeholders, including regulators, suppliers, and environmental organizations. Volkswagen actively engaged with these stakeholders, seeking their input and expertise to develop effective solutions. By fostering collaboration and partnerships, Volkswagen demonstrated a willingness to work together with others to address the crisis and create a more sustainable future.

In conclusion, Volkswagen's crisis management provides valuable lessons for companies facing similar challenges. Transparency and accountability, effective communication, swift action and remediation, learning from mistakes, strengthening corporate governance, rebuilding trust and reputation, and collaboration and partnerships are all essential elements of successful crisis management. By applying these lessons, companies can navigate crises more effectively, protect their reputation, and emerge stronger and more resilient.

Rana

7.1 The Rana Family Journey

The Rana family has a remarkable journey that has led them to establish a pasta empire known as Rana. Their story is one of passion, innovation, and determination. Guido Rana, the founder of the company, started his business in the small Italian town of Verona in 1962. What began as a small pasta shop has now grown into a global brand, with Rana products being enjoyed by millions of people around the world.

7.1.1 From Humble Beginnings

Guido Rana's journey began with a simple dream: to create the finest pasta using traditional Italian techniques. He started by making fresh pasta by hand and selling it to local customers. Guido's commitment to quality and his dedication to preserving the authentic taste of Italian pasta quickly gained him a loyal customer base.

7.1.2 Innovation and Expansion

As the demand for Rana's pasta grew, Guido realized the need to innovate and expand his business. He introduced new pasta varieties, experimenting with different flavors and ingredients. This commitment to innovation allowed Rana to stand out in a crowded market and attract a wider customer base.

Guido also recognized the importance of expanding beyond the local market. He invested in state-of-the-art production facilities and developed efficient distribution networks to reach customers across

Italy and eventually internationally. This expansion strategy enabled Rana to become a household name not only in Italy but also in many countries around the world.

7.1.3 Family Dynamics in Rana's Business

One of the key factors behind Rana's success is the strong presence of family dynamics within the business. Guido Rana's children, Gian Luca and Matteo, joined the company and brought fresh perspectives and ideas. They embraced their father's vision and worked together to take Rana to new heights.

The Rana family's close-knit relationship and shared values have played a crucial role in the company's growth. They have fostered a culture of trust, collaboration, and mutual respect, which has allowed them to make important decisions collectively and navigate challenges effectively.

7.1.4 Key Takeaways from Rana's Growth

Rana's journey holds valuable lessons for other companies, regardless of their sector, size, or leadership structure. Here are some key takeaways:

1. Commitment to Quality: Rana's unwavering commitment to producing the highest quality pasta has been a cornerstone of their success. Companies can learn the importance of prioritizing quality in their products or services to build a strong reputation and customer loyalty.

2. Innovation and Adaptability: Rana's willingness to innovate and adapt to changing market demands has allowed them to stay ahead of the competition. Companies should continuously seek new ways to improve their offerings and be open to embracing change to remain relevant in a dynamic business environment.

3. Family Values and Collaboration: The Rana family's strong bond and collaborative approach have been instrumental in their success. Companies can benefit from fostering a culture of trust, open communication, and shared values, which can lead to better decision-making and a more cohesive work environment.

4. Global Expansion: Rana's strategic approach to expanding beyond their local market has enabled them to reach a wider customer base. Companies should consider exploring opportunities for international growth and invest in building efficient distribution networks to expand their reach.

5. Customer-Centric Approach: Rana's focus on meeting customer needs and preferences has been a driving force behind their success. Companies should prioritize understanding their customers and delivering products or services that exceed their expectations.

In conclusion, the Rana family's journey from a small pasta shop to a global pasta empire is a testament to the power of passion, innovation, and family values. Their success story offers valuable insights for other companies looking to achieve sustainable growth and build a strong brand presence. By embracing quality, innovation, collaboration, global expansion, and a customer-centric approach, companies can learn from Rana's journey and pave their path to success.

7.2 Innovation and Expansion in Rana's Success

Rana, a family-owned pasta company, has achieved remarkable success through its innovative approach and strategic expansion. This section will delve into the key factors that have contributed to Rana's growth and how other companies can learn from their achievements.

7.2.1 A Legacy of Innovation

Rana's success story began with Giovanni Rana, who started making fresh pasta in his small kitchen in Verona, Italy, in the 1960s. From the very beginning, Rana focused on innovation, constantly seeking ways to improve the quality and taste of their products. Giovanni Rana's passion for pasta and his commitment to excellence laid the foundation for the company's future success.

7.2.2 Diversification and Market Expansion

One of the key strategies that propelled Rana's growth was their ability to diversify their product offerings and expand into new markets. While initially specializing in fresh pasta, Rana recognized the changing consumer preferences and expanded their range to include sauces, ready meals, and other related products. This diversification allowed Rana to cater to a wider customer base and capture new market segments.

Furthermore, Rana's expansion into international markets played a crucial role in their success. By identifying opportunities in foreign markets and adapting their products to suit local tastes and preferences, Rana was able to establish a global presence. Their commitment to quality and authenticity resonated with consumers worldwide, enabling them to become a leader in the pasta industry.

7.2.3 Embracing Technology and Automation

Rana's success can also be attributed to their embrace of technology and automation in their production processes. By investing in state-of-the-art machinery and automation systems, Rana was able to increase efficiency, reduce costs, and maintain consistent product quality. This technological advancement allowed them to meet the growing demand for their products while ensuring that their traditional recipes and artisanal techniques were preserved.

7.2.4 Family Values and Entrepreneurial Spirit

As a family-owned company, Rana's success is deeply rooted in their strong family values and entrepreneurial spirit. The Rana family has maintained a hands-on approach to the business, ensuring that their passion and commitment are reflected in every aspect of the company's operations. This familial involvement has fostered a culture of innovation, adaptability, and long-term thinking, which has been instrumental in Rana's sustained growth.

7.2.5 Sustainability and Social Responsibility

Rana recognizes the importance of sustainability and social responsibility in today's business landscape. They have implemented various initiatives to reduce their environmental impact, such as optimizing energy consumption, minimizing waste, and sourcing ingredients responsibly. Rana's commitment to sustainability not only aligns with their values but also resonates with consumers who prioritize ethical and environmentally friendly products.

Furthermore, Rana actively engages with the local communities where they operate, supporting initiatives that promote education, health, and social welfare. By integrating sustainability and social responsibility into their business practices, Rana has not only enhanced their brand reputation but also contributed to the well-being of society.

7.2.6 Lessons for Other Companies

Rana's success offers valuable lessons for other companies looking to innovate and expand their operations:

1. **Embrace innovation:** Constantly seek ways to improve your products or services. Innovation is key to staying ahead of the

competition and meeting evolving customer needs.

2. **Diversify strategically:** Explore opportunities to diversify your product offerings and expand into new markets. This can help you reach a broader customer base and mitigate risks associated with relying on a single product or market.

3. **Leverage technology:** Embrace technology and automation to increase efficiency, reduce costs, and maintain product quality. Technology can be a powerful tool in scaling your operations and meeting growing demand.

4. **Preserve core values:** Maintain a strong connection to your company's core values and heritage. This can foster a sense of purpose and guide decision-making, even as the company grows and evolves.

5. **Prioritize sustainability:** Incorporate sustainable practices into your business operations. Consumers are increasingly conscious of environmental and social issues, and aligning your company with sustainable practices can enhance your brand reputation and attract socially responsible consumers.

6. **Engage with the community:** Actively participate in initiatives that benefit the communities where you operate. Building strong relationships with local stakeholders

can create a positive impact and contribute to long-term success.

By studying the success of Rana and other family companies, businesses from various sectors can gain insights into the strategies and values that have propelled these companies to greatness. The power of family companies lies not only in their ability to innovate and expand but also in their commitment to preserving their heritage and making a positive impact on society.

7.3 Family Dynamics in Rana's Business

Family dynamics play a crucial role in the success of a family business, and Rana is no exception. As a family-owned pasta empire, Rana has thrived by leveraging the unique strengths and dynamics that come with being a family-run company. In this section, we will explore the key aspects of family dynamics that have contributed to Rana's business success.

7.3.1 Shared Vision and Values

One of the fundamental aspects of Rana's success lies in the shared vision and values that the family members hold. The Rana family has a deep-rooted passion for creating high-quality pasta products that bring joy to people's lives. This shared vision has guided their decision-making and strategic direction, ensuring that every aspect of the business aligns with their core values.

The Rana family's commitment to excellence and their unwavering dedication to producing authentic Italian pasta has set them apart from their

competitors. This shared vision has not only helped them maintain a strong brand identity but has also allowed them to build a loyal customer base that values their commitment to quality.

7.3.2 Strong Family Bonds and Trust

Family businesses often benefit from the strong bonds and trust that exist among family members. In the case of Rana, the family's close-knit relationships have played a significant role in their success. The Rana family members trust and support each other, creating a harmonious working environment that fosters collaboration and innovation.

The trust among family members has allowed them to make important business decisions with confidence. They can rely on each other's expertise and judgment, which has enabled them to navigate challenges and seize opportunities effectively. This level of trust has also extended to their employees, creating a positive work culture that promotes loyalty and dedication.

7.3.3 Succession Planning and Continuity

Successful family businesses understand the importance of succession planning and ensuring continuity across generations. Rana has excelled in this aspect by implementing a well-defined succession plan that ensures a smooth transition of leadership and responsibilities.

The Rana family has carefully groomed the next generation to take over the reins of the business. They have provided them with the necessary education, training, and exposure to different aspects of the company's operations. This approach has allowed the younger generation to develop a deep understanding of the business while also bringing fresh perspectives and ideas.

By ensuring a seamless transition of leadership, Rana has been able to maintain its core values and business strategies while adapting to changing market dynamics. This continuity has been instrumental in their long-term success and has helped them build a legacy that extends beyond a single generation.

7.3.4 Open Communication and Conflict Resolution

Effective communication and conflict resolution are vital in any business, but they become even more critical in a family-run company. Rana has fostered a culture of open communication, where family members and employees feel comfortable expressing their ideas, concerns, and feedback.

The Rana family recognizes the importance of addressing conflicts promptly and constructively. They have established clear channels of communication and have implemented mechanisms to resolve conflicts in a fair and transparent manner. This approach has helped them maintain a healthy work environment and has prevented conflicts from escalating and affecting the business's overall performance.

7.3.5 Balancing Family and Business

One of the unique challenges of family businesses is finding the right balance between family dynamics and business operations. Rana has successfully

managed this delicate balance by establishing clear boundaries and roles within the family.

The Rana family understands the importance of separating family matters from business decisions. They have implemented robust governance structures and professional management practices to ensure that business decisions are made based on merit and strategic considerations rather than personal relationships.

By maintaining a professional approach to business operations, Rana has been able to make objective decisions that drive the company's growth and success. This balance has allowed them to leverage the strengths of both family and non-family members, creating a diverse and dynamic team.

7.3.6 Embracing Innovation and Adaptability

Rana's success can also be attributed to their ability to embrace innovation and adapt to changing market trends. The family's entrepreneurial spirit and willingness to take calculated risks have allowed them to stay ahead of the competition.

The Rana family encourages a culture of innovation within the company, where new ideas are welcomed and nurtured. They have invested in research and development, continuously exploring new flavors, ingredients, and production techniques to meet evolving consumer demands.

Furthermore, Rana has demonstrated adaptability by expanding their product offerings and exploring new markets. They have successfully introduced ready-to-eat meals and expanded their presence globally, catering to the changing lifestyles and preferences of consumers.

7.3.7 Conclusion

Rana's success as a family business can be attributed to the strong family dynamics that underpin their operations. Their shared vision and values, strong family bonds, effective communication, and conflict resolution, along with a well-executed succession plan, have contributed to their long-term success.

By balancing family and business, embracing innovation, and adapting to market changes, Rana has been able to build a thriving pasta empire. Other companies can learn from Rana's family dynamics by fostering a shared vision, promoting open communication, and embracing innovation while maintaining a strong commitment to their core values.

7.4 Key Takeaways from Rana's Growth

Rana, a family-owned pasta company, has experienced remarkable growth and success over the years. From its humble beginnings as a small business to becoming a pasta empire, Rana's journey holds valuable lessons for other companies looking to achieve similar growth and success. In this section, we will explore the key takeaways from Rana's growth and how other companies can apply these lessons to their own strategies.

7.4.1 Embrace Innovation and Expansion

One of the key factors behind Rana's growth is their commitment to innovation and expansion. Rana

continuously seeks new ways to improve their products, processes, and market reach. They have introduced innovative pasta flavors, shapes, and packaging, catering to the evolving tastes and preferences of their customers. Rana has also expanded their product line to include ready-made meals and sauces, diversifying their offerings and capturing a larger market share.

The lesson here is for companies to embrace innovation and constantly seek ways to improve their products and services. By staying ahead of the curve and adapting to changing market demands, companies can position themselves for growth and success.

7.4.2 Maintain a Strong Focus on Quality

Rana has built a reputation for delivering high-quality pasta products. They prioritize the use of fresh and premium ingredients, ensuring that their pasta is not only delicious but also of superior quality. Rana's commitment to quality has earned them the trust and loyalty of their customers, allowing them to establish a strong market presence.

Other companies can learn from Rana's emphasis on quality. By prioritizing quality in their products and services, companies can differentiate themselves from competitors and build a loyal customer base.

7.4.3 Preserve Family Values and Culture

Family values and culture play a significant role in Rana's business. The Rana family has instilled a sense of tradition, authenticity, and passion into their company. They have maintained a hands-on approach to their business, ensuring that their family values are reflected in every aspect of their operations. This commitment to their heritage has not only helped Rana maintain its unique identity but has also resonated with customers who appreciate the authenticity and tradition behind the brand.

For other companies, preserving and promoting their own unique values and culture can be a powerful differentiator. By staying true to their roots and incorporating their values into their business practices, companies can create a strong brand identity and connect with their target audience on a deeper level.

7.4.4 Foster Strong Family Dynamics

Rana's success can be attributed, in part, to the strong family dynamics within the company. The Rana family has effectively leveraged their collective strengths and expertise to drive the company forward. They have established clear roles and responsibilities, ensuring that each family member contributes their unique skills to the business. This collaborative approach has allowed Rana to make informed decisions, navigate challenges, and capitalize on opportunities effectively.

Companies can learn from Rana's approach to family dynamics by fostering strong relationships and collaboration within their own teams. By leveraging the diverse skills and perspectives of their employees, companies can enhance their problem-solving capabilities and drive innovation.

7.4.5 Build Strong Relationships with Suppliers and Partners

Rana recognizes the importance of building strong relationships with their suppliers and partners. They work closely with local farmers to source the freshest ingredients, ensuring the quality and sustainability of their products. Rana also collaborates with retailers and distributors to expand their market reach and ensure their products are readily available to customers.

The lesson here is for companies to prioritize building strong relationships with their suppliers and partners. By fostering mutually beneficial partnerships, companies can enhance their supply chain efficiency, access new markets, and create a competitive advantage.

7.4.6 Adapt to Changing Consumer Preferences

Rana has successfully adapted to changing consumer preferences and market trends. They have introduced healthier options, such as whole wheat and gluten-free pasta, to cater to the growing demand for healthier food choices. Rana has also embraced convenience by offering ready-made meals and sauces, providing customers with quick and easy meal solutions.

Companies can learn from Rana's ability to adapt to changing consumer preferences. By staying attuned to market trends and consumer demands, companies can proactively adjust their offerings and stay ahead of the competition.

7.4.7 Invest in Marketing and Branding

Rana understands the importance of effective marketing and branding. They have invested in building a strong brand image, leveraging their family heritage, and emphasizing the quality and authenticity of their products. Rana's marketing efforts have helped them create brand recognition and establish a loyal customer base.

Other companies can learn from Rana's approach to marketing and branding. By investing in strategic marketing initiatives and building a compelling brand story, companies can enhance their visibility, attract customers, and differentiate themselves in the market.

In conclusion, Rana's growth and success can be attributed to their commitment to innovation, quality, family values, strong family dynamics, partnerships, adaptability, and effective marketing. By applying these key takeaways to their own strategies, companies in various sectors and sizes can position themselves for growth and success.

Benetton

8.1 The Benetton Family Legacy

The Benetton family has left an indelible mark on the fashion industry, not only through their iconic brand but also through their commitment to diversity and social impact. The story of the Benetton family is one of innovation, creativity, and a deep understanding of the power of branding.

8.1.1 The Origins of Benetton

The Benetton family's journey began in 1965 when Luciano Benetton and his siblings, Giuliana, Gilberto, and Carlo, founded the Benetton Group in Ponzano Veneto, Italy. What started as a small knitwear company quickly grew into a global fashion empire, known for its vibrant colors and bold designs.

8.1.2 Benetton's Approach to Fashion and Design

One of the key factors that set Benetton apart from its competitors was its unique approach to fashion and design. The company embraced a philosophy of inclusivity and diversity, using its clothing as a canvas to promote social issues and spark conversations. Benetton's iconic advertisements featuring people from different backgrounds and cultures became a hallmark of their brand.

Benetton's commitment to innovation extended beyond their designs. They were one of the first fashion companies to adopt a vertically integrated business model, controlling every aspect of the production process, from manufacturing to retail.

This allowed them to maintain strict quality control and respond quickly to changing market trends.

8.1.3 Social Responsibility in Benetton's Business

The Benetton family recognized the importance of social responsibility early on and integrated it into their business practices. They established the Benetton Foundation in 1987, which focused on promoting social issues such as human rights, education, and cultural diversity. Through their foundation, they supported numerous projects and initiatives around the world, making a positive impact on communities.

Furthermore, Benetton was one of the first fashion companies to prioritize sustainability and environmental responsibility. They implemented eco-friendly practices in their production processes and actively sought out sustainable materials. By doing so, they not only reduced their environmental footprint but also set an example for other companies in the industry.

8.1.4 Lessons in Branding from Benetton

Benetton's success can be attributed, in large part, to their mastery of branding. They understood that a strong brand identity could differentiate them from their competitors and create a loyal customer base. Here are some key lessons that other companies can learn from the Benetton family's approach to branding:

1. **Embrace diversity:** Benetton's advertisements featuring people from different backgrounds and cultures resonated

with consumers worldwide. By celebrating diversity, companies can connect with a broader audience and foster inclusivity.

2. **Take a stand:** Benetton used their brand as a platform to address social issues. Companies that align themselves with causes they believe in can build a strong emotional connection with their customers and create a sense of purpose.

3. **Innovate and adapt:** Benetton's ability to stay ahead of trends and constantly innovate allowed them to remain relevant in a fast-paced industry. Companies should continuously seek new ways to improve their products, processes, and customer experiences.

4. **Integrate sustainability:** As consumers become more conscious of their environmental impact, companies that prioritize sustainability will have a competitive advantage. By adopting eco-friendly practices and promoting sustainable values, companies can attract environmentally conscious customers.

5. **Tell a compelling story:** Benetton's advertisements told powerful stories that resonated with people. Companies should strive to create a narrative around their brand that engages customers on an emotional level and leaves a lasting impression.

The Benetton family's legacy in the fashion industry is a testament to the power of innovation, social responsibility, and effective branding. Their ability to create a global brand that stands for more than just fashion has left a lasting impact on the industry. By embracing diversity, taking a stand, and prioritizing sustainability, companies can learn valuable lessons from the Benetton family's success.

8.2 Benetton's Approach to Fashion and Design

Benetton is a renowned Italian fashion brand that has made a significant impact on the industry with its unique approach to fashion and design. The company was founded by the Benetton family in 1965 and has since become a global leader in the fashion industry. Benetton's success can be attributed to its innovative designs, commitment to social responsibility, and effective branding strategies. In this section, we will explore Benetton's approach to fashion and design and the lessons that other companies can learn from their success.

8.2.1 Innovative and Diverse Designs

One of the key factors that set Benetton apart from its competitors is its innovative and diverse designs. The company has always been known for its bold use of colors and unconventional patterns, which have become synonymous with the brand. Benetton's designers have a keen eye for trends and a willingness to take risks, resulting in collections that are both unique and appealing to a wide range of customers.

Other companies can learn from Benetton's approach to design by embracing creativity and thinking outside the box. By pushing boundaries and experimenting with new ideas, companies can differentiate themselves in the market and attract a loyal customer base. Benetton's success demonstrates the importance of staying ahead of trends and constantly evolving to meet the changing demands of consumers.

8.2.2 Social Responsibility and Ethical Practices

Benetton has been a pioneer in incorporating social responsibility and ethical practices into its business model. The company has consistently advocated for social causes and used its platform to raise awareness about important issues. Benetton's campaigns have tackled topics such as diversity, human rights, and environmental sustainability, making a significant impact on society.

Other companies can learn from Benetton's commitment to social responsibility by aligning their business practices with their values. By taking a stand on important issues and implementing ethical practices, companies can build a positive brand image and gain the trust and loyalty of customers. Benetton's success demonstrates that businesses can make a difference in the world while also achieving financial success.

8.2.3 Effective Branding Strategies

Benetton is known for its strong and distinctive brand identity. The company has successfully positioned itself as a brand that stands for diversity, inclusivity, and social change. Benetton's iconic advertisements, featuring people from different backgrounds and cultures, have become instantly recognizable and have helped to reinforce the brand's values and message.

Other companies can learn from Benetton's branding strategies by developing a clear and compelling brand identity. By understanding their target audience and effectively communicating their brand values, companies can create a strong emotional connection with customers. Benetton's success demonstrates the power of storytelling and using branding as a tool to create a meaningful and lasting impression.

8.2.4 Collaboration and Partnerships

Benetton has also been successful in forming collaborations and partnerships with other brands and designers. These collaborations have allowed Benetton to tap into new markets and reach a wider audience. By partnering with designers and artists who share their vision, Benetton has been able to create unique and limited-edition collections that generate excitement and drive sales.

Other companies can learn from Benetton's approach to collaboration by seeking out strategic partnerships that can enhance their brand and expand their reach. By joining forces with complementary brands or influencers, companies can leverage each other's strengths and create mutually beneficial opportunities. Benetton's success demonstrates the power of collaboration in driving innovation and growth.

In conclusion, Benetton's approach to fashion and design has been instrumental in their success as a family company. Their innovative designs, commitment to social responsibility, effective branding strategies, and collaborations have set them apart in the fashion industry. Other companies can learn from Benetton by embracing creativity, incorporating social responsibility into their business practices, developing a strong brand identity, and seeking out strategic partnerships. By adopting these principles, companies can position themselves for long-term success and make a positive impact on society.

8.3 Social Responsibility in Benetton's Business

Benetton, a renowned Italian fashion brand, has not only made a name for itself in the fashion industry but has also become a symbol of social responsibility. The company's commitment to social causes and its innovative approach to addressing global issues have set it apart from its competitors. In this section, we will explore how Benetton incorporates social responsibility into its business practices and the lessons that other companies can learn from its success.

8.3.1 A Holistic Approach to Social Responsibility

Benetton's approach to social responsibility goes beyond mere philanthropy or corporate social responsibility initiatives. The company believes in taking a holistic approach that integrates social and environmental concerns into its core business strategy. Benetton recognizes that its success is intertwined with the well-being of society and the environment, and therefore, it actively works towards creating a positive impact.

8.3.2 Promoting Diversity and Inclusion

One of the key aspects of Benetton's social responsibility is its commitment to promoting diversity and inclusion. The company has been a pioneer in featuring models from diverse backgrounds in its advertising campaigns, challenging traditional beauty standards and promoting inclusivity. By doing so, Benetton has not only gained recognition for its bold and inclusive marketing but has also contributed to the broader conversation on diversity and representation in the fashion industry.

8.3.3 Ethical Supply Chain Practices

Benetton understands the importance of ensuring ethical practices throughout its supply chain. The company has implemented strict guidelines and standards to ensure that its suppliers adhere to fair labor practices, environmental sustainability, and human rights. By actively monitoring its supply chain, Benetton aims to create a positive impact on the lives of workers and communities involved in the production process.

8.3.4 Environmental Sustainability

Benetton recognizes the urgent need to address environmental challenges and has taken significant steps towards sustainability. The company has implemented various initiatives to reduce its carbon footprint, minimize waste, and promote responsible consumption. Benetton's commitment to sustainability is evident in its use of eco-friendly materials, energy-efficient production processes, and recycling programs. By prioritizing environmental sustainability, Benetton not only contributes to a greener future but also appeals to environmentally conscious consumers.

8.3.5 Collaboration and Partnerships

Benetton understands that addressing complex social and environmental issues requires collaboration and partnerships. The company actively seeks collaborations with NGOs, government agencies, and other stakeholders to leverage their expertise and resources. By working together, Benetton aims to create innovative solutions and drive positive change on a larger scale. This collaborative approach not only enhances the effectiveness of their initiatives but also strengthens their reputation as a socially responsible brand.

8.3.6 Transparency and Accountability

Transparency and accountability are crucial elements of Benetton's social responsibility practices. The company believes in being open and honest about its actions, progress, and challenges. Benetton regularly publishes sustainability reports, detailing its efforts, achievements, and areas for improvement. By being transparent, Benetton builds trust with its stakeholders and invites feedback, enabling continuous improvement in its social responsibility initiatives.

Benetton's social responsibility practices offer valuable lessons for other companies:

1. **Integrate social responsibility into the core business strategy:** Companies should view social responsibility as an integral part of their business strategy rather than a separate initiative. By aligning social and environmental concerns with their core operations, companies can create a sustainable and impactful approach.

2. **Promote diversity and inclusion:** Embracing diversity and promoting inclusivity can not only enhance a company's brand image but also contribute to a more equitable society. Companies should strive to represent diverse perspectives and challenge societal norms through their marketing and hiring practices.

3. **Ensure ethical supply chain practices:** Companies should prioritize ethical sourcing and fair labor practices throughout their supply chains. By actively monitoring and engaging with suppliers, companies can create positive change and mitigate risks associated with unethical practices.

4. **Embrace environmental sustainability:** Environmental sustainability should be a priority for companies across industries. By implementing eco-friendly practices, reducing waste, and promoting responsible

consumption, companies can contribute to a greener future while appealing to environmentally conscious consumers.

5. **Collaborate and form partnerships:** Addressing complex social and environmental challenges requires collaboration and partnerships. Companies should seek opportunities to collaborate with stakeholders, leveraging their expertise and resources to drive meaningful change.

6. **Emphasize transparency and accountability:** Transparency builds trust and accountability ensures continuous improvement. Companies should be transparent about their social responsibility efforts, share progress, and invite feedback from stakeholders.

By adopting these lessons from Benetton's social responsibility practices, companies can not only contribute to a better world but also enhance their brand reputation, attract socially conscious consumers, and drive long-term success.

8.4 Lessons in Branding from Benetton

Branding is a crucial aspect of any successful company, and Benetton is a prime example of a family company that has mastered the art of branding. With its unique approach to fashion, diversity, and social impact, Benetton has created a strong and recognizable brand identity that has resonated with consumers worldwide. In this section, we will explore the lessons in branding that other companies can learn from Benetton's success.

8.4.1 Embrace Controversy and Take a Stand

One of the key lessons in branding from Benetton is the importance of embracing controversy and taking a stand on social issues. Benetton has never shied away from addressing sensitive topics through its advertising campaigns. By tackling issues such as racism, social inequality, and environmental concerns, Benetton has positioned itself as a brand that is not afraid to challenge the status quo. This approach has not only generated significant media attention but has also helped Benetton connect with consumers who value brands that stand for something beyond just selling products.

8.4.2 Create a Strong Visual Identity

Benetton is known for its bold and vibrant use of colors in its branding and advertising. The company has created a strong visual identity that is instantly recognizable and sets it apart from its competitors. By consistently using bright and eye-catching colors in its clothing, store designs, and marketing materials, Benetton has created a unique and memorable brand image. This lesson highlights the importance of developing a visual identity that aligns with the company's values and resonates with its target audience.

8.4.3 Tell Compelling Stories

Benetton has mastered the art of storytelling in its branding efforts. Through its advertising campaigns, the company tells powerful and thought-provoking stories that evoke emotions and create a connection with consumers. By focusing on real people and their experiences, Benetton has been able to create a sense of authenticity and empathy, which has resonated with its audience. This lesson emphasizes the importance of storytelling in branding and how it can help companies build a strong emotional connection with their customers.

8.4.4 Foster Diversity and Inclusion

Benetton has long been a champion of diversity and inclusion, both in its branding and within the company itself. The company's advertising campaigns have featured models from different ethnicities, backgrounds, and body types, promoting a message of acceptance and inclusivity. By embracing diversity, Benetton has been able to appeal to a wide range of consumers and create a brand that is seen as progressive and forward-thinking. This lesson highlights the importance of fostering diversity and inclusion in branding efforts to attract a diverse customer base.

8.4.5 Align Brand Values with Business Practices

Benetton's commitment to social responsibility and ethical practices is not just a marketing ploy but is deeply ingrained in the company's business practices. The company has implemented sustainable and environmentally friendly initiatives throughout its supply chain, ensuring that its brand values align with its actions. This lesson emphasizes the importance of aligning brand values with business practices to build trust and credibility with consumers.

8.4.6 Collaborate with Influencers and Partners

Benetton has successfully collaborated with influencers, artists, and other brands to create unique and impactful campaigns. By partnering with individuals and organizations that share its values and vision, Benetton has been able to amplify its message and reach a wider audience. This lesson highlights the power of collaboration in branding and how it can help companies expand their reach and influence.

8.4.7 Stay Relevant and Evolve with the Times

One of the key lessons in branding from Benetton is the importance of staying relevant and evolving with the times. The company has continuously adapted its branding and marketing strategies to reflect changing consumer preferences and societal trends. By staying ahead of the curve and embracing innovation, Benetton has remained a relevant and influential brand in the fashion industry. This lesson emphasizes the need for companies to be flexible and adaptable in their branding efforts to stay competitive in a rapidly changing market.

In conclusion, Benetton's success in branding can be attributed to its willingness to embrace controversy, create a strong visual identity, tell compelling stories, foster diversity and inclusion, align brand values with business practices, collaborate with influencers and partners, and stay relevant and evolve with the times. These lessons in branding can be applied by other companies, regardless of their sector, size, or leadership, to create a strong and impactful brand

that resonates with consumers and drives business
success.

Zanussi

9.1 The Zanussi Family Story

The Zanussi family has a rich history in the home appliance industry, and their story is a testament to the power of innovation and adaptability. Founded in 1916 by Antonio Zanussi in Pordenone, Italy, Zanussi started as a small workshop producing wood-burning ovens. Over the years, the company expanded its product range and became a leading player in the European home appliance market.

9.1.1 From Humble Beginnings to Industry Leader

Antonio Zanussi's entrepreneurial spirit and commitment to quality laid the foundation for the success of the Zanussi brand. He believed in creating products that would make people's lives easier and more comfortable. With this vision in mind, Zanussi began manufacturing gas and electric stoves, refrigerators, and washing machines.

Under the leadership of Antonio's son, Lino Zanussi, the company experienced significant growth and expansion. Lino recognized the importance of innovation and invested heavily in research and development. This led to the introduction of several groundbreaking products, such as the first gas cooker with an electric ignition system and the first fully automatic washing machine.

9.1.2 Embracing Technological Advancements

One of the key factors that set Zanussi apart from its competitors was its ability to embrace technological advancements. The company was quick to adopt new

technologies and incorporate them into its product offerings. For example, Zanussi was one of the first companies to introduce electronic controls in its appliances, making them more user-friendly and efficient.

Zanussi also recognized the importance of design in creating a competitive edge. The company collaborated with renowned designers to create aesthetically pleasing and functional appliances that appealed to consumers. This focus on design helped Zanussi establish itself as a premium brand in the home appliance market.

9.1.3 Family Values and Long-Term Vision

Throughout its history, the Zanussi family has remained committed to its core values of integrity, quality, and customer satisfaction. These values have been passed down through generations and continue to guide the company's operations. The Zanussi family's long-term vision and commitment to excellence have played a crucial role in the company's success.

Family involvement has also been a significant factor in Zanussi's achievements. The family's deep understanding of the business and industry has allowed them to make informed decisions and navigate through challenges effectively. Their hands-on approach and personal commitment to the company's success have fostered a culture of dedication and innovation within the organization.

9.1.4 Lessons for Other Companies

Zanussi's success holds valuable lessons for other companies, regardless of their industry or size. Here are some key takeaways:

1. Embrace innovation: Zanussi's ability to embrace new technologies and incorporate them into their products has been instrumental in their success. Companies should continuously seek ways to innovate and stay ahead of the competition.

2. Focus on design: Zanussi's collaboration with designers helped them create products that not only performed well but also appealed to consumers aesthetically. Investing in design can give companies a competitive edge and enhance their brand image.

3. Maintain strong core values: Zanussi's commitment to integrity, quality, and customer satisfaction has been a driving force behind their success. Companies should establish and uphold strong core values that guide their decision-making and operations.

4. Foster a culture of innovation: Zanussi's family involvement and hands-on approach have fostered a culture of dedication and innovation within the organization. Companies should encourage and empower their employees to think creatively and contribute to the company's growth.

5. Adapt to changing market dynamics: Zanussi's ability to adapt to changing market

dynamics and consumer preferences has allowed them to stay relevant over the years. Companies should be agile and willing to evolve their strategies to meet the ever-changing demands of the market.

6. Invest in research and development: Zanussi's investment in research and development has been crucial in driving product innovation. Companies should allocate resources to research and development to stay at the forefront of technological advancements in their industry.

In conclusion, the Zanussi family's story is a testament to the power of innovation, adaptability, and strong family values. Their ability to embrace new technologies, focus on design, and maintain a long-term vision has propelled them to become a leader in the home appliance industry. Other companies can learn from Zanussi's success by embracing innovation, fostering a culture of creativity, and staying true to their core values.

9.2 Zanussi's Innovation in Home Appliances

Zanussi, a renowned Italian home appliance manufacturer, has established itself as a leader in the industry through its relentless pursuit of innovation. With a rich family legacy and a commitment to excellence, Zanussi has consistently pushed the boundaries of technology and design to create appliances that enhance the lives of consumers around the world. In this section, we will explore Zanussi's innovative approach to home appliances and the valuable lessons that other companies can learn from their success.

9.2.1 A Legacy of Innovation

Zanussi's journey began in 1916 when Antonio Zanussi founded the company in Pordenone, Italy. From its inception, Zanussi focused on developing innovative solutions to meet the evolving needs of households. The company quickly gained recognition for its commitment to quality and technological advancements, setting the stage for its future success.

One of Zanussi's early breakthroughs came in the 1950s when it introduced the first gas-powered refrigerator in Europe. This innovation revolutionized the way people stored and preserved food, making it more accessible and convenient. Zanussi continued to build on this success by introducing a range of innovative appliances, including washing machines, dishwashers, and ovens, that transformed the way people managed their households.

9.2.2 Embracing Technological Advancements

Zanussi's commitment to innovation is deeply rooted in its ability to embrace technological advancements. The company has consistently invested in research and development to stay at the forefront of the industry. By leveraging emerging technologies, Zanussi has been able to introduce groundbreaking features and functionalities in its appliances.

For example, Zanussi was one of the first companies to incorporate digital controls and sensors in its appliances, allowing for precise temperature regulation and energy efficiency. This not only enhanced the performance of their products but also provided consumers with greater control and convenience. Zanussi's ability to adapt to new technologies and integrate them seamlessly into their appliances has been a key driver of their success.

9.2.3 Design and User Experience

In addition to technological advancements, Zanussi places a strong emphasis on design and user experience. The company understands that appliances are not just functional tools but also an integral part of the home environment. Zanussi's appliances are designed with a focus on aesthetics, ergonomics, and ease of use, ensuring that they seamlessly integrate into any kitchen or laundry room.

By prioritizing user experience, Zanussi has been able to create appliances that are intuitive and user-friendly. From innovative control panels to thoughtful storage solutions, Zanussi's appliances are designed to simplify everyday tasks and enhance the overall user experience. This customer-centric approach has not only earned Zanussi a loyal customer base but has also set a benchmark for other companies in the industry.

9.2.4 Sustainability and Energy Efficiency

Zanussi recognizes the importance of sustainability and energy efficiency in today's world. The company is committed to reducing its environmental impact by developing appliances that are energy-efficient

and eco-friendly. Zanussi's appliances are designed to minimize water and energy consumption without compromising on performance.

By incorporating advanced technologies such as intelligent sensors and eco-cycles, Zanussi's appliances optimize resource usage and reduce waste. This commitment to sustainability not only aligns with the growing consumer demand for eco-friendly products but also positions Zanussi as a responsible and forward-thinking company.

9.2.5 Lessons for Other Companies

Zanussi's success in the home appliance industry offers valuable lessons for other companies looking to thrive in their respective sectors:

1. **Embrace innovation:** Zanussi's relentless pursuit of innovation has allowed them to stay ahead of the competition. Companies should invest in research and development to continuously improve their products and services.

2. **Adapt to new technologies:** By embracing emerging technologies, companies can unlock new possibilities and create products that meet the changing needs of consumers.

3. **Prioritize design and user experience:** Aesthetics and user-friendliness play a crucial role in attracting and retaining customers. Companies should focus on creating products that are visually appealing, ergonomic, and easy to use.

4. **Commit to sustainability:** In today's environmentally conscious world, companies must prioritize sustainability and develop eco-friendly solutions. This not only benefits the planet but also resonates with consumers who are increasingly seeking sustainable options.

5. **Invest in research and development:** Zanussi's commitment to research and development has been instrumental in their success. Companies should allocate resources to stay at the forefront of their industries and drive innovation.

By incorporating these lessons into their business strategies, companies can learn from Zanussi's innovative approach and position themselves for long-term success in their respective industries. Zanussi's legacy of innovation, commitment to excellence, and customer-centric approach serve as a testament to the power of family companies in driving industry-wide transformation.

9.3 Family Values in Zanussi's Business Strategy

Family values play a crucial role in shaping the business strategies of successful family companies. Zanussi, a renowned name in the home appliance industry, is no exception. With a rich family legacy and a commitment to innovation and adaptability, Zanussi has thrived in a competitive market. In this section, we will explore how family values have influenced Zanussi's business strategy and what other companies can learn from their approach.

9.3.1 A Strong Sense of Purpose

One of the key aspects of Zanussi's business strategy is their strong sense of purpose, which is deeply rooted in their family values. The Zanussi family has always believed in providing high-quality home appliances that enhance the lives of their customers. This commitment to improving the daily lives of people has guided their product development and innovation efforts.

By aligning their business goals with their core values, Zanussi has been able to create a strong brand identity and establish a loyal customer base. Other companies can learn from Zanussi's approach by identifying their own core values and integrating them into their business strategies. This not only helps in building a strong brand but also fosters a sense of purpose and direction within the organization.

9.3.2 Long-Term Perspective

Family companies often have the advantage of taking a long-term perspective, as they are not driven solely by short-term financial gains. Zanussi has embraced this approach by focusing on sustainable growth and long-term success rather than quick profits. This long-term perspective allows them to make strategic decisions that may not yield immediate results but contribute to the company's overall growth and stability.

By prioritizing long-term goals, Zanussi has been able to invest in research and development, innovation, and employee development. This has enabled them to stay ahead of the competition and

adapt to changing market trends. Other companies can learn from Zanussi's long-term perspective by avoiding short-sighted decisions and investing in strategies that will yield sustainable growth in the future.

9.3.3 Strong Family Governance

Family governance is a critical aspect of Zanussi's business strategy. The Zanussi family has established a robust governance structure that ensures effective decision-making and smooth succession planning. By maintaining a balance between family involvement and professional management, Zanussi has been able to leverage the strengths of both family members and external professionals.

The family governance structure at Zanussi promotes transparency, accountability, and open communication among family members and key stakeholders. This allows for the efficient resolution of conflicts and the alignment of business objectives. Other companies can learn from Zanussi's approach by implementing effective governance structures that strike a balance between family dynamics and professional management.

9.3.4 Employee Engagement and Development

Zanussi recognizes the importance of its employees in driving the company's success. They have fostered a culture of employee engagement, empowerment, and continuous development. By investing in their employees' growth and well-being, Zanussi has created a motivated and dedicated workforce.

The family values of trust, respect, and collaboration are deeply ingrained in Zanussi's organizational culture. This encourages employees to take ownership of their work, contribute innovative ideas, and work together towards common goals. Other companies can learn from Zanussi's approach by prioritizing employee engagement, providing opportunities for growth, and fostering a positive work environment.

9.3.5 Customer-Centric Approach

Zanussi's business strategy revolves around meeting the needs and expectations of their customers. They have a deep understanding of their target market and continuously strive to deliver products that exceed customer expectations. Zanussi's commitment to customer satisfaction has earned them a strong reputation and a loyal customer base.

By adopting a customer-centric approach, Zanussi has been able to build long-lasting relationships with their customers. They actively seek feedback, listen to customer preferences, and incorporate them into their product development process. Other companies can learn from Zanussi's customer-centric approach by prioritizing customer satisfaction, investing in market research, and continuously improving their products and services.

9.3.6 Innovation and Adaptability

Zanussi's success can be attributed to their ability to innovate and adapt to changing market dynamics. They have consistently introduced new technologies, designs, and features in their home appliances to stay ahead of the competition. Zanussi's commitment to innovation has allowed them to meet evolving customer needs and preferences.

Furthermore, Zanussi has demonstrated a willingness to adapt their business strategies to emerging trends and challenges. They have embraced digital transformation, sustainability initiatives, and new business models to remain relevant in a rapidly changing industry. Other companies can learn from Zanussi's focus on innovation and adaptability by fostering a culture of continuous improvement, embracing new technologies, and being open to change.

In conclusion, Zanussi's business strategy is deeply influenced by their family values. Their strong sense of purpose, long-term perspective, effective family governance, employee engagement, customer-centric approach, and focus on innovation and adaptability have been instrumental in their success. Other companies can learn from Zanussi's approach by aligning their business strategies with their core values, adopting a long-term perspective, implementing effective governance structures, prioritizing employee engagement and customer satisfaction, and embracing innovation and adaptability. By incorporating these principles, companies can enhance their competitiveness and achieve sustainable growth.

9.4 Applying Zanussi's Adaptability to Other Industries

Zanussi, a renowned family company in the home appliance industry, has demonstrated remarkable adaptability throughout its history. This adaptability

has allowed them to navigate changing market dynamics, embrace innovation, and stay ahead of the competition. Zanussi's ability to adapt can serve as a valuable lesson for companies in various industries looking to thrive in a rapidly evolving business landscape.

9.4.1 Embracing Change and Innovation

One of the key aspects of Zanussi's adaptability is their willingness to embrace change and innovation. They have consistently demonstrated a forward-thinking approach, constantly seeking new ways to improve their products and processes. Zanussi's commitment to innovation has allowed them to stay relevant and competitive in an industry that is constantly evolving.

Companies in other industries can learn from Zanussi's approach by fostering a culture of innovation within their organizations. By encouraging employees to think creatively and explore new ideas, companies can stay ahead of the curve and adapt to changing customer needs and preferences. Embracing change and innovation can help companies remain agile and responsive in a rapidly changing business environment.

9.4.2 Customer-Centric Approach

Zanussi has always prioritized the needs and preferences of their customers. They have consistently strived to understand their customers' requirements and deliver products that meet and exceed their expectations. This customer-centric approach has allowed Zanussi to build strong relationships with their customers and establish a loyal customer base.

Other companies can learn from Zanussi's customer-centric approach by placing a strong emphasis on understanding their target market and tailoring their products and services accordingly. By actively listening to customer feedback and incorporating it into their business strategies, companies can build strong customer relationships and create products that truly resonate with their target audience.

9.4.3 Flexibility and Agility

Zanussi's adaptability is also evident in their ability to be flexible and agile in response to market changes. They have shown a willingness to adjust their strategies and operations to meet new challenges and seize emerging opportunities. This flexibility has allowed them to successfully navigate industry disruptions and maintain their competitive edge.

Companies in other industries can learn from Zanussi's flexibility by being open to change and willing to adjust their strategies when necessary. By staying attuned to market trends and being proactive in their decision-making, companies can position themselves for success even in the face of uncertainty. Being flexible and agile enables companies to adapt to changing market conditions and seize new opportunities as they arise.

9.4.4 Strong Leadership and Family Values

Zanussi's success can also be attributed to their strong leadership and adherence to family values.

The company has been guided by a clear vision and a strong sense of purpose, which has helped them navigate challenges and make strategic decisions. Zanussi's commitment to their core values has fostered a sense of unity and purpose within the organization, driving their success.

Other companies can learn from Zanussi's strong leadership and family values by cultivating a strong company culture and aligning their actions with their core values. By providing clear direction and fostering a sense of purpose, leaders can inspire their teams to adapt and thrive in a rapidly changing business environment. Additionally, upholding family values such as trust, integrity, and collaboration can create a strong foundation for success.

9.4.5 Collaboration and Partnerships

Zanussi has also demonstrated the importance of collaboration and partnerships in driving adaptability. They have actively sought collaborations with other companies, research institutions, and industry experts to leverage their expertise and stay at the forefront of innovation. By forging strategic partnerships, Zanussi has been able to access new markets, technologies, and ideas, enhancing their adaptability.

Companies in other industries can learn from Zanussi's approach by actively seeking collaborations and partnerships that can enhance their adaptability. By leveraging the expertise and resources of external partners, companies can gain access to new knowledge, technologies, and markets.

Collaboration can foster innovation, drive growth, and enhance a company's ability to adapt to changing market dynamics.

In conclusion, Zanussi's adaptability has been a key factor in their success as a family company in the home appliance industry. Their ability to embrace change and innovation, adopt a customer-centric approach, be flexible and agile, uphold strong leadership and family values, and foster collaborations and partnerships has allowed them to thrive in a rapidly evolving business landscape. Companies in other industries can learn valuable lessons from Zanussi's adaptability and apply them to their own strategies to stay competitive and succeed in their respective markets.

Diesel

10.1 The Diesel Family Legacy

Diesel is a renowned Italian fashion brand known for its unique and rebellious style. Founded by Renzo Rosso in 1978, Diesel has become a global icon in the fashion industry. The success of Diesel can be attributed to the strong influence of the Diesel family, who have played a significant role in shaping the brand's identity and creative direction.

10.1.1 The Origins of Diesel

The Diesel family legacy began with the vision and entrepreneurial spirit of Renzo Rosso. Born in the small town of Brugine, Italy, Renzo had a passion for fashion from a young age. After completing his studies in textile manufacturing, he started working for a clothing manufacturer. However, he soon realized that he wanted to create something unique and innovative.

In 1978, Renzo Rosso founded Diesel, a brand that would challenge the conventions of the fashion industry. The name "Diesel" was chosen to represent the energy and power associated with the fuel, reflecting the brand's rebellious and unconventional nature.

10.1.2 Diesel's Unique Branding and Marketing

One of the key factors that set Diesel apart from its competitors is its unique branding and marketing strategies. The Diesel family understood the importance of creating a distinct brand identity that resonated with their target audience.

Diesel's marketing campaigns have always been bold, provocative, and unconventional. The brand has embraced controversial themes and challenged societal norms, creating a sense of rebellion and individuality. This approach has helped Diesel establish a strong and loyal customer base who identify with the brand's values and attitude.

Furthermore, Diesel has been successful in leveraging the power of storytelling in its marketing efforts. The brand has created narratives that go beyond selling products, focusing on creating emotional connections with its customers. By telling compelling stories, Diesel has been able to engage its audience on a deeper level and build a strong brand community.

10.1.3 Family Influence in Diesel's Creative Direction

The Diesel family has played a crucial role in shaping the brand's creative direction. Renzo Rosso's entrepreneurial spirit and passion for innovation have been instrumental in driving Diesel's success. As the founder and creative director, Renzo has been actively involved in the design process, ensuring that the brand stays true to its rebellious and edgy aesthetic.

Moreover, Renzo's family members have also contributed to Diesel's creative direction. His son, Stefano Rosso, joined the company in 2003 and has been involved in various aspects of the business, including product development and marketing. Stefano's fresh perspective and understanding of the younger generation have helped Diesel stay relevant and connected to its target audience.

The Diesel family's involvement in the creative process has allowed the brand to maintain its authenticity and originality. By staying true to their vision and values, Diesel has been able to differentiate itself in a highly competitive industry.

10.1.4 Lessons in Brand Identity from Diesel

There are several valuable lessons that other companies can learn from Diesel's success in building a strong brand identity:

1. Embrace uniqueness and individuality: Diesel's success lies in its ability to embrace individuality and challenge the status quo. Companies should strive to create a brand identity that is distinct and resonates with their target audience.

2. Be bold and provocative: Diesel's marketing campaigns have always been bold and provocative, capturing the attention of consumers. Companies should not be afraid to take risks and push boundaries in their marketing efforts.

3. Tell compelling stories: Diesel has mastered the art of storytelling, creating narratives that go beyond selling products. Companies should focus on creating emotional connections with their customers through storytelling.

4. Involve the family in the creative process: The Diesel family's involvement in the creative direction of the brand has been crucial to its success. Companies should consider involving

family members who share the same vision and values in key decision-making processes.

5.   Stay true to your vision and values: Diesel has stayed true to its rebellious and edgy aesthetic throughout the years. Companies should remain authentic and consistent in their brand messaging to build trust and loyalty among customers.

In conclusion, the Diesel family legacy has played a significant role in shaping the brand's identity and success. Through their unique branding and marketing strategies, Diesel has been able to differentiate itself in the fashion industry. Other companies can learn valuable lessons from Diesel's approach to building a strong brand identity that resonates with their target audience.

10.2 Diesel's Unique Branding and Marketing

Diesel, the Italian fashion brand founded by Renzo Rosso in 1978, has become synonymous with creativity, rebellion, and a distinct brand identity. With its innovative marketing strategies and bold advertising campaigns, Diesel has successfully carved out a unique position in the fashion industry. In this section, we will explore Diesel's approach to branding and marketing and the lessons that other companies can learn from their success.

10.2.1 The Birth of a Brand

Diesel's journey began with a rebellious spirit and a desire to challenge the status quo. Renzo Rosso, the founder of Diesel, recognized the need for a brand that would resonate with the youth culture of the time. He wanted to create a brand that stood out from the crowd and embraced individuality. This vision laid the foundation for Diesel's unique branding and marketing strategies.

10.2.2 Embracing Creativity and Innovation

One of the key elements of Diesel's success is its ability to embrace creativity and innovation in its branding and marketing efforts. The brand has consistently pushed boundaries and challenged conventional norms through its advertising campaigns. Diesel's advertisements have often been provocative, controversial, and thought-provoking, capturing the attention of consumers and generating buzz around the brand.

By taking risks and thinking outside the box, Diesel has been able to create a distinct brand identity that resonates with its target audience. The brand's ability to tap into the zeitgeist and connect with consumers on an emotional level has been instrumental in its success.

10.2.3 Authenticity and Storytelling

Diesel's success can also be attributed to its commitment to authenticity and storytelling. The brand has always stayed true to its roots and maintained a strong sense of identity. Diesel's advertising campaigns often tell compelling stories that evoke emotions and create a connection with consumers.

By weaving narratives into its marketing efforts, Diesel has been able to create a sense of authenticity and build a loyal customer base. The brand's

storytelling approach has allowed it to go beyond selling products and create a lifestyle that consumers aspire to be a part of.

10.2.4 Engaging with the Consumer

Diesel understands the importance of engaging with its consumers and building a community around the brand. The company has leveraged social media platforms and digital marketing to connect with its target audience on a deeper level. Diesel's social media presence is characterized by its witty and irreverent tone, which resonates with its young and fashion-forward consumers.

The brand has also embraced experiential marketing, organizing events and collaborations that allow consumers to interact with the brand in a meaningful way. By creating memorable experiences, Diesel has been able to foster a sense of loyalty and advocacy among its customers.

10.2.5 Lessons for Other Companies

There are several key lessons that other companies can learn from Diesel's unique branding and marketing strategies:

1. Embrace creativity and innovation: Companies should not be afraid to take risks and think outside the box. By pushing boundaries and challenging norms, brands can create a distinct identity that sets them apart from competitors.

2. Stay true to your roots: Authenticity is crucial in building a strong brand. Companies should

stay true to their values and maintain a consistent brand identity that resonates with consumers.

3. Tell compelling stories: Storytelling is a powerful tool in marketing. By creating narratives that evoke emotions and connect with consumers, brands can build a deeper connection and foster loyalty.

4. Engage with consumers: Building a community around the brand is essential. Companies should leverage social media and digital marketing to engage with their target audience and create meaningful experiences.

5. Be bold and irreverent: Taking a bold and irreverent approach can help brands stand out and capture the attention of consumers. Companies should not be afraid to challenge conventions and embrace their unique voice.

Diesel's success in branding and marketing can be attributed to its ability to embrace creativity, authenticity, and storytelling. By staying true to its rebellious spirit and engaging with its consumers, Diesel has created a brand that is not only recognized for its fashion-forward designs but also for its unique identity. Other companies can learn from Diesel's approach and apply these lessons to their own branding and marketing strategies to differentiate themselves in the market.

10.3 Family Influence in Diesel's Creative Direction

Family businesses often have a unique advantage when it comes to creative direction. The close-knit nature of family dynamics allows for a deep understanding of the brand's values, vision, and heritage. Diesel, a renowned Italian fashion brand, is a prime example of how family influence can shape and drive creative direction within a company.

10.3.1 The Diesel Family Legacy

Diesel was founded in 1978 by Renzo Rosso, who still serves as the company's President. Renzo's entrepreneurial spirit and passion for denim laid the foundation for Diesel's success. From the beginning, Renzo instilled a sense of rebellion and non-conformity into the brand's DNA, which continues to be a driving force behind Diesel's creative direction.

10.3.2 Diesel's Unique Branding and Marketing

One of the key aspects of Diesel's success lies in its unique branding and marketing strategies. The company has always been known for its provocative and edgy advertising campaigns that challenge societal norms. This distinctive approach has allowed Diesel to stand out in a crowded fashion industry and attract a loyal customer base.

The family's influence in Diesel's creative direction is evident in the brand's ability to consistently push boundaries and take risks. Renzo Rosso's vision and values have shaped the brand's identity, allowing it

to maintain a rebellious and unconventional image throughout the years.

10.3.3 Family Influence in Diesel's Creative Direction

The family's involvement in Diesel goes beyond just the founder. Renzo Rosso has actively involved his children in the business, allowing them to contribute their unique perspectives and talents to the creative direction of the brand. This multi-generational collaboration has helped Diesel stay relevant and innovative in an ever-changing fashion landscape.

The family's deep understanding of Diesel's heritage and values has allowed them to maintain a consistent creative direction while also adapting to evolving consumer trends. Their hands-on approach ensures that the brand's identity remains intact, even as new ideas and concepts are explored.

10.3.4 Lessons in Brand Identity from Diesel

Other companies can learn valuable lessons from Diesel's approach to creative direction and brand identity. Here are some key takeaways:

1. Embrace your brand's heritage and values:

Diesel's success lies in its ability to stay true to its rebellious and non-conformist roots. Companies should embrace their unique heritage and values, as these can serve as a strong foundation for creative direction.

2. Foster a culture of innovation and risk-taking:

Diesel's willingness to take risks and push boundaries has allowed the brand to stay ahead of

the curve. Encouraging a culture of innovation and experimentation can lead to fresh and exciting creative directions.

3. Involve the family in decision-making:

Family businesses have the advantage of close-knit relationships and shared values. Involving family members in the creative direction can bring a deep understanding of the brand's identity and ensure its continuity across generations.

4. Stay true to your brand's identity:

While it's important to adapt to changing consumer preferences, it's equally crucial to stay true to your brand's core identity. Diesel's consistent rebellious image has resonated with its target audience and set it apart from competitors.

5. Continuously evolve and adapt:

Creative direction should not be stagnant. Companies should be open to evolving and adapting their strategies to stay relevant in a dynamic market. Diesel's ability to balance tradition with innovation has allowed it to remain a leader in the fashion industry.

In conclusion, Diesel's success in creative direction can be attributed to the family's deep understanding of the brand's heritage, values, and vision. Their ability to embrace innovation, take risks, and stay true to the brand's identity has set Diesel apart in the fashion industry. Other companies can learn from Diesel's approach by embracing their own brand's heritage, fostering a culture of innovation, involving the family in decision-making, staying true to their brand's identity, and continuously evolving and adapting to market trends.

10.4 Lessons in Brand Identity from Diesel

Brand identity is a crucial aspect of any successful company. It is the unique combination of elements that sets a brand apart from its competitors and creates a lasting impression on consumers. Diesel, the renowned Italian fashion brand, has mastered the art of brand identity and offers valuable lessons for other companies looking to establish a strong and recognizable brand.

10.4.1 Embrace Unconventional and Edgy Branding

One of the key lessons that companies can learn from Diesel is the importance of embracing unconventional and edgy branding. Diesel has built its brand identity around rebellion, creativity, and non-conformity. From its provocative advertising campaigns to its bold and innovative designs, Diesel has consistently pushed the boundaries of traditional fashion branding.

By embracing unconventional branding strategies, Diesel has been able to capture the attention of its target audience and create a strong emotional connection with them. This approach has allowed the brand to stand out in a crowded market and attract a loyal customer base.

10.4.2 Tell a Compelling Brand Story

Another lesson that companies can learn from Diesel is the power of storytelling in building a brand

identity. Diesel has successfully crafted a compelling brand story that resonates with its target audience. The brand's story revolves around the idea of individuality, self-expression, and breaking free from societal norms.

Through its marketing campaigns and brand messaging, Diesel has effectively communicated its brand story to consumers, creating a sense of authenticity and emotional connection. By telling a compelling brand story, companies can differentiate themselves from their competitors and establish a strong brand identity that resonates with consumers.

10.4.3 Consistency in Brand Messaging

Consistency is key when it comes to building a strong brand identity, and Diesel understands this well. The brand has consistently maintained its rebellious and edgy image across all touchpoints, from its product designs to its marketing campaigns. This consistency has helped Diesel establish a clear and recognizable brand identity that consumers can easily identify with.

Companies can learn from Diesel's approach by ensuring that their brand messaging is consistent across all channels and platforms. Consistency in brand messaging helps to build trust and credibility among consumers, and it reinforces the brand's values and positioning in the market.

10.4.4 Engage with the Target Audience

Diesel has successfully engaged with its target audience by creating experiences that go beyond traditional marketing. The brand has organized events, collaborations, and partnerships that resonate with its target audience and align with its brand values. By actively engaging with its customers, Diesel has been able to foster a sense of community and loyalty among its fan base.

Companies can learn from Diesel's approach by finding innovative ways to engage with their target audience. This could include hosting events, creating interactive content, or collaborating with influencers or like-minded brands. By actively engaging with their customers, companies can build a strong brand community and foster long-term customer loyalty.

10.4.5 Adapt to Changing Consumer Preferences

Another valuable lesson from Diesel is the importance of adapting to changing consumer preferences. The fashion industry is constantly evolving, and Diesel has successfully navigated these changes by staying attuned to the needs and desires of its target audience.

Diesel has embraced sustainability and ethical practices in response to the growing demand for environmentally conscious fashion. The brand has also embraced digital transformation by leveraging technology to enhance the customer experience and reach a wider audience.

Companies can learn from Diesel's ability to adapt by staying agile and responsive to changing consumer preferences. By continuously monitoring market trends and consumer behavior, companies can make informed decisions and evolve their brand identity to stay relevant in a dynamic business landscape.

10.4.6 Authenticity and Transparency

Authenticity and transparency are essential elements of Diesel's brand identity. The brand has consistently communicated its values and beliefs to consumers, and it has been transparent about its manufacturing processes and sustainability initiatives.

Companies can learn from Diesel's commitment to authenticity and transparency by being open and honest with their customers. By communicating their brand values and being transparent about their practices, companies can build trust and credibility among consumers, which is crucial for long-term success.

10.4.7 Stay True to Your Brand DNA

Lastly, Diesel's success in brand identity can be attributed to its ability to stay true to its brand DNA. Despite evolving trends and changing consumer preferences, Diesel has remained true to its rebellious and edgy image. The brand has successfully adapted without compromising its core values and brand identity.

Companies can learn from Diesel's approach by staying true to their brand DNA and core values. While it is important to adapt and evolve, it is equally important to maintain a consistent brand identity that resonates with consumers.

In conclusion, Diesel's success in brand identity can be attributed to its embrace of unconventional branding, compelling storytelling, consistency in brand messaging, engagement with the target audience, adaptation to changing consumer preferences, authenticity and transparency, and staying true to its brand DNA. By learning from these lessons, companies can establish a strong and recognizable brand identity that sets them apart from their competitors and resonates with consumers.

Luxottica

11.1 The Luxottica Family Journey

Luxottica is a shining example of a family company that has achieved remarkable success in the eyewear industry. Founded in 1961 by Leonardo Del Vecchio, Luxottica has grown to become the world's largest eyewear company, dominating the market with its iconic brands such as Ray-Ban and Oakley. The Luxottica family's journey is a testament to their vision, determination, and commitment to excellence.

11.1.1 From Humble Beginnings to Global Dominance

The Luxottica story began in a small town in Italy, where Leonardo Del Vecchio started his career as an apprentice in a tool and die factory. With a strong work ethic and a passion for precision, Del Vecchio honed his skills and eventually ventured into the eyewear industry. In 1961, he founded Luxottica, initially specializing in the production of components for eyeglasses.

Through relentless dedication and a keen understanding of the market, Luxottica gradually expanded its operations and began manufacturing complete eyewear frames. The company's commitment to quality and innovation quickly gained recognition, and Luxottica started collaborating with renowned fashion brands to produce exclusive eyewear collections.

11.1.2 Vertical Integration: A Strategic Advantage

One of the key factors behind Luxottica's success is its vertical integration strategy. The company controls every aspect of the eyewear production process, from design and manufacturing to distribution and retail. By owning the entire value chain, Luxottica has achieved unparalleled control over its products, ensuring consistent quality and timely delivery.

Luxottica's vertical integration also allows the company to maintain a strong competitive advantage. By eliminating intermediaries and streamlining operations, Luxottica can offer a wide range of eyewear products at various price points, catering to different consumer segments. This flexibility has enabled Luxottica to adapt to changing market trends and maintain its market leadership.

11.1.3 Family Values at the Core

At the heart of Luxottica's success lies its strong adherence to family values. The Luxottica family has instilled a culture of integrity, collaboration, and long-term thinking within the company. This family-centric approach has fostered a sense of loyalty and commitment among employees, creating a cohesive and motivated workforce.

The Luxottica family's involvement in the business has also played a crucial role in shaping the company's direction. Their deep understanding of the industry, combined with their entrepreneurial spirit, has guided Luxottica's strategic decisions and fueled its growth. The family's hands-on approach and personal commitment to excellence have set the standard for the entire organization.

11.1.4 Lessons Learned from Luxottica's Success

Luxottica's journey offers valuable insights for other companies striving for success. Here are some key lessons that can be learned from Luxottica's achievements:

1. Embrace Vertical Integration: By controlling the entire value chain, companies can ensure quality, efficiency, and flexibility in their operations. Vertical integration allows for greater control over product development, manufacturing, and distribution, leading to a competitive advantage in the market.

2. Cultivate a Strong Company Culture: Family companies have a unique advantage in fostering a strong company culture based on shared values and a long-term perspective. By nurturing a sense of belonging and purpose among employees, companies can create a motivated workforce that is committed to achieving excellence.

3. Focus on Innovation and Adaptability: Luxottica's success can be attributed, in part, to its ability to innovate and adapt to changing market trends. Companies should prioritize continuous improvement, invest in research and development, and stay ahead of the curve to remain competitive in today's dynamic business environment.

4. Build Strong Relationships: Luxottica's collaborations with renowned fashion brands have been instrumental in its success. Building strong partnerships and nurturing relationships with key stakeholders can open doors to new opportunities and enhance brand reputation.

5. Maintain a Long-Term Perspective: Family companies often have a long-term vision that extends beyond immediate financial gains. By focusing on sustainable growth and maintaining a commitment to quality, companies can build a solid foundation for long-term success.

In conclusion, Luxottica's journey exemplifies the power of family companies to achieve remarkable success. Through vertical integration, a strong company culture, and a focus on innovation, Luxottica has become a global leader in the eyewear industry. Other companies can learn valuable lessons from Luxottica's story and apply them to their own businesses, regardless of sector, size, or leadership structure.

11.2 Luxottica's Vertical Integration Strategy

Luxottica is a renowned Italian eyewear company that has achieved remarkable success through its unique vertical integration strategy. This strategy involves controlling every aspect of the eyewear production process, from design and manufacturing to distribution and retail. By maintaining control over the entire value chain, Luxottica has been able to establish itself as a dominant player in the eyewear industry and create a strong competitive advantage. In this section, we will explore Luxottica's vertical integration strategy and the key takeaways that other companies can learn from its success.

11.2.1 The Power of Vertical Integration

Vertical integration refers to the process of owning and controlling multiple stages of the production and distribution process within an industry. Luxottica's vertical integration strategy is based on the belief that by controlling every aspect of the eyewear business, they can ensure quality, efficiency, and innovation throughout the entire value chain. This approach has allowed Luxottica to differentiate itself from its competitors and maintain a strong market position.

11.2.2 Design and Manufacturing Excellence

Luxottica's vertical integration begins with its strong focus on design and manufacturing. The company has a dedicated team of designers who create innovative and stylish eyewear collections that cater to different market segments and consumer preferences. By having an in-house design team, Luxottica can quickly respond to changing fashion trends and customer demands, giving them a competitive edge in the market.

In terms of manufacturing, Luxottica operates a vast network of production facilities around the world. This extensive manufacturing capability allows them to have full control over the production process, ensuring high-quality standards and efficient operations. Luxottica's manufacturing expertise also enables them to produce eyewear for other luxury brands through licensing agreements, further expanding their market reach and revenue streams.

11.2.3 Distribution and Retail Dominance

Luxottica's vertical integration extends to its distribution and retail operations. The company owns a vast network of retail stores, including well-known brands like Sunglass Hut and LensCrafters. This extensive retail presence gives Luxottica direct access to consumers and allows them to showcase their eyewear collections in a controlled environment. By owning their retail outlets, Luxottica can provide a seamless customer experience and build strong brand loyalty.

Furthermore, Luxottica has established strategic partnerships with major optical retailers and department stores worldwide. These partnerships enable Luxottica to distribute their eyewear through a wide range of channels, reaching a diverse customer base. By controlling the distribution process, Luxottica can ensure that their products are readily available to consumers, further strengthening their market position.

11.2.4 Key Takeaways from Luxottica's Success

Luxottica's vertical integration strategy offers valuable insights and lessons for other companies, regardless of their industry or size. Here are some key takeaways:

1. **Control the Value Chain**: By owning and controlling multiple stages of the production and distribution process, companies can ensure quality, efficiency, and innovation throughout the entire value chain. This level of control can provide a competitive

advantage and enhance customer satisfaction.

2. **Invest in Design and Manufacturing**: Investing in design and manufacturing capabilities allows companies to create innovative and high-quality products that meet customer demands. By having an in-house design team and manufacturing facilities, companies can respond quickly to market trends and maintain control over product quality.

3. **Build a Strong Retail Presence**: Owning retail outlets or establishing strategic partnerships with retailers can provide companies with direct access to consumers and help build brand loyalty. A strong retail presence allows companies to showcase their products in a controlled environment and provide a seamless customer experience.

4. **Establish Strategic Partnerships**: Collaborating with other industry players can expand market reach and distribution channels. Strategic partnerships can help companies tap into new customer segments and increase brand visibility.

5. **Embrace Innovation**: Continuous innovation is crucial for staying ahead in a competitive market. Companies should invest in research and development to create new products, improve existing ones, and adapt to changing customer preferences.

6. **Maintain a Customer-Centric Approach**: Putting the customer at the center of business operations is essential for long-term success. Companies should strive to understand customer needs and preferences, and tailor their products and services accordingly.

In conclusion, Luxottica's vertical integration strategy has been instrumental in its success as a global eyewear powerhouse. By controlling every aspect of the eyewear production process, from design and manufacturing to distribution and retail, Luxottica has created a strong competitive advantage and established itself as a market leader. Other companies can learn from Luxottica's approach by focusing on vertical integration, investing in design and manufacturing, building a strong retail presence, establishing strategic partnerships, embracing innovation, and maintaining a customer-centric approach.

11.3 Family Values in Luxottica's Business Model

Luxottica, a leading eyewear company, has achieved remarkable success through its unique business model and strong adherence to family values. The company's commitment to its core principles has played a significant role in its growth and dominance in the eyewear industry. In this section, we will explore the importance of family values in Luxottica's business model and the lessons that other companies can learn from their success.

11.3.1 A Family-Centric Approach

Luxottica's foundation is built on family values, which have been deeply ingrained in the company's culture since its inception. The company was founded by Leonardo Del Vecchio, who started his career as an apprentice in a small eyewear factory. His humble beginnings and strong work ethic laid the groundwork for Luxottica's family-centric approach.

Family values are at the core of Luxottica's decision-making processes and business strategies. The company places a strong emphasis on fostering a sense of unity, trust, and loyalty among its employees, suppliers, and customers. This family-oriented approach has created a strong bond within the organization and has contributed to its long-term success.

11.3.2 Long-Term Vision and Stability

One of the key aspects of Luxottica's business model is its long-term vision and stability. The company has always focused on sustainable growth and has avoided short-term gains that could compromise its core values. Luxottica's commitment to maintaining its family-owned status has allowed it to make strategic decisions that prioritize long-term success over immediate profits.

Luxottica's long-term vision is reflected in its approach to product development, brand partnerships, and market expansion. The company invests heavily in research and development to ensure the highest quality and innovation in its eyewear products. By forging strategic partnerships with renowned fashion brands, Luxottica has been able to expand its market reach and maintain its position as a global leader in the eyewear industry.

11.3.3 Strong Corporate Governance

Luxottica's success can also be attributed to its strong corporate governance, which is deeply rooted in family values. The company has implemented a robust governance structure that ensures transparency, accountability, and ethical practices. Luxottica's board of directors includes both family members and independent professionals, creating a balanced decision-making process that combines family wisdom with external expertise.

The company's commitment to strong corporate governance has helped it navigate challenges and maintain its reputation as a trustworthy and reliable business partner. Luxottica's adherence to ethical practices and responsible business conduct has earned the trust and loyalty of its stakeholders, including customers, employees, and investors.

11.3.4 Employee Engagement and Development

Luxottica recognizes the importance of its employees in driving its success. The company places a strong emphasis on employee engagement, development, and well-being. Luxottica's family-oriented culture fosters a sense of belonging and encourages employees to take pride in their work.

The company invests in training and development programs to enhance the skills and knowledge of its employees. Luxottica also provides opportunities for career growth and advancement, creating a sense of loyalty and commitment among its workforce. By prioritizing employee engagement and development, Luxottica has built a strong and dedicated team that is instrumental in achieving its business objectives.

11.3.5 Customer-Centric Approach

Luxottica's commitment to delivering exceptional customer experiences is another key aspect of its business model. The company understands the importance of building strong relationships with its customers and strives to exceed their expectations at every touchpoint.

Luxottica's customer-centric approach is reflected in its product offerings, personalized services, and innovative retail experiences. The company leverages its deep understanding of customer preferences and market trends to create eyewear collections that resonate with its target audience. Luxottica's retail stores provide a welcoming and immersive environment where customers can explore and try on a wide range of eyewear options.

11.3.6 Lessons for Other Companies

Luxottica's success offers valuable lessons for other companies, regardless of their sector, size, or leadership structure. Here are some key takeaways:

1. Embrace family values: Incorporate family values into your company's culture and decision-making processes. Foster a sense of unity, trust, and loyalty among your employees, suppliers, and customers.

2. Prioritize long-term vision: Focus on sustainable growth and avoid short-term

gains that may compromise your core values. Make strategic decisions that prioritize long-term success over immediate profits.

3. Implement strong corporate governance: Establish a robust governance structure that ensures transparency, accountability, and ethical practices. Combine family wisdom with external expertise to make balanced and informed decisions.

4. Invest in employee engagement and development: Recognize the importance of your employees in driving your success. Invest in their training, development, and well-being to create a loyal and committed workforce.

5. Adopt a customer-centric approach: Prioritize delivering exceptional customer experiences. Understand your customers' preferences and create products and services that exceed their expectations.

By incorporating these lessons into their business models, companies can foster a strong sense of purpose, build lasting relationships with stakeholders, and achieve sustainable growth. Luxottica's success serves as a testament to the power of family values in driving business excellence.

11.4 Key Takeaways from Luxottica's Success

Luxottica is a prime example of a family company that has achieved remarkable success in the eyewear industry. With its vertical integration strategy and

strong commitment to family values, Luxottica has become a dominant force in the market. There are several key takeaways that other companies can learn from Luxottica's success.

11.4.1 Embrace Vertical Integration

One of the most significant factors contributing to Luxottica's success is its vertical integration strategy. Luxottica controls every aspect of its supply chain, from design and manufacturing to distribution and retail. By owning its production facilities, retail stores, and even licensing agreements with luxury brands, Luxottica has gained a competitive advantage in the eyewear industry. This level of control allows Luxottica to ensure quality, maintain consistency, and respond quickly to market demands. Other companies can learn from Luxottica's approach by considering the benefits of vertical integration in their own industries.

11.4.2 Focus on Branding and Licensing

Luxottica has successfully built a portfolio of iconic eyewear brands, including Ray-Ban, Oakley, and Persol, among others. By investing in strong branding and licensing agreements, Luxottica has been able to capture a significant share of the global eyewear market. Other companies can learn from Luxottica's emphasis on brand building and licensing as a means to differentiate themselves and expand their market presence.

11.4.3 Prioritize Innovation and Design

Luxottica understands the importance of innovation and design in the highly competitive fashion industry. The company continuously invests in research and development to create innovative eyewear designs that appeal to consumers. Luxottica's commitment to staying ahead of trends and constantly pushing the boundaries of eyewear design has helped it maintain its position as a market leader. Other companies can learn from Luxottica's focus on innovation and design by prioritizing creativity and staying attuned to evolving customer preferences.

11.4.4 Nurture a Strong Company Culture

Family values are deeply ingrained in Luxottica's company culture. The company places a strong emphasis on teamwork, respect, and integrity, which are values that have been passed down through generations. Luxottica's commitment to fostering a positive work environment and nurturing its employees has contributed to its success. Other companies can learn from Luxottica's focus on building a strong company culture that aligns with their core values and promotes employee engagement and satisfaction.

11.4.5 Adapt to Changing Market Conditions

Luxottica has demonstrated its ability to adapt to changing market conditions and consumer preferences. The company has successfully expanded its product offerings beyond traditional eyewear to include prescription lenses, sunglasses, and even smart eyewear. Luxottica's willingness to embrace new technologies and adapt its business model has allowed it to stay relevant and meet the evolving needs of its customers. Other companies can learn from Luxottica's agility and willingness to embrace change as a means to stay competitive in dynamic markets.

11.4.6 Foster Strong Relationships with Suppliers and Retail Partners

Luxottica recognizes the importance of building strong relationships with its suppliers and retail partners. The company works closely with its suppliers to ensure the highest quality materials and manufacturing processes. Luxottica also maintains strong partnerships with retailers worldwide, allowing it to effectively distribute its products and reach a global customer base. Other companies can learn from Luxottica's focus on collaboration and building mutually beneficial relationships with suppliers and retail partners.

11.4.7 Invest in Corporate Social Responsibility

Luxottica understands the significance of corporate social responsibility and actively invests in initiatives that benefit the communities it operates in. The company has implemented various sustainability programs, including reducing its environmental footprint and promoting ethical sourcing. Luxottica's commitment to social responsibility not only aligns with its core values but also resonates with consumers who increasingly prioritize ethical and sustainable practices. Other companies can learn from Luxottica's dedication to corporate social responsibility and the positive impact it can have on both society and business.

11.4.8 Continuously Improve Customer Experience

Luxottica places a strong emphasis on providing an exceptional customer experience. The company invests in training its employees to deliver personalized service and ensures that its retail stores offer a welcoming and engaging environment for customers. Luxottica's focus on customer satisfaction has helped it build a loyal customer base and drive repeat business. Other companies can learn from Luxottica's commitment to continuously improving the customer experience by investing in training, enhancing store environments, and prioritizing customer satisfaction.

In conclusion, Luxottica's success can be attributed to its vertical integration strategy, strong branding and licensing, focus on innovation and design, nurturing a strong company culture, adaptability, fostering strong relationships, investing in corporate social responsibility, and continuously improving the customer experience. These key takeaways can serve as valuable lessons for other companies looking to achieve long-term success in their respective industries. By incorporating these principles into their business strategies, companies can position themselves for growth, differentiation, and sustainability.

Maina

12.1 The Maina Family Legacy

The Maina family legacy is a testament to the power of tradition, quality, and artisanal excellence. For over a century, the Maina family has been at the forefront of the baking industry, creating delicious and authentic Italian baked goods that have captured the hearts and taste buds of people around the world. Their commitment to preserving traditional baking methods and using only the finest ingredients has set them apart from their competitors and ensured their continued success.

12.1.1 A Rich History

The Maina family's journey in the baking industry began in the late 1800s when Giovanni Maina opened a small bakery in the Piedmont region of Italy. With a passion for baking and a dedication to quality, Giovanni quickly gained a reputation for his delicious bread and pastries. As the demand for his products grew, Giovanni's sons, Luigi and Carlo, joined the family business, expanding its reach and establishing Maina as a household name in Italy.

12.1.2 Commitment to Traditional Baking

One of the key factors that have contributed to Maina's success is their unwavering commitment to traditional baking methods. While many companies have embraced modern technology and automation, Maina has stayed true to their roots, preserving the time-honored techniques that have been passed down through generations. From hand-kneading the

dough to using stone ovens, Maina ensures that each product is crafted with care and attention to detail.

This commitment to tradition not only sets Maina apart from their competitors but also resonates with consumers who appreciate the authenticity and craftsmanship that goes into each bite. It is this dedication to preserving the art of traditional baking that has allowed Maina to maintain a loyal customer base and establish themselves as a trusted brand in the industry.

12.1.3 Family Involvement in Quality Control

Another key aspect of Maina's success is the active involvement of the Maina family in quality control. As a family-owned and operated business, the Maina family takes great pride in ensuring that every product that bears their name meets their high standards of excellence. From selecting the finest ingredients to overseeing the baking process, the Maina family is involved in every step of the production process.

This hands-on approach to quality control allows Maina to maintain consistency and ensure that each product meets their exacting standards. It also allows them to quickly address any issues that may arise and make necessary adjustments to maintain the quality that their customers have come to expect. By maintaining a close connection to their products, the Maina family can guarantee that each item that leaves their bakery is of the highest quality.

12.1.4 Lessons in Artisanal Excellence

Maina's success offers valuable lessons for other companies, regardless of their industry or size. Here are some key takeaways:

1. Embrace tradition: While innovation is important, there is also value in preserving traditional methods and techniques. Maina's commitment to traditional baking has helped them stand out in a crowded market and attract customers who appreciate the authenticity and craftsmanship of their products.

2. Focus on quality: Quality should always be a top priority. By maintaining strict quality control measures and actively involving the family in the process, Maina ensures that their products consistently meet their high standards. This attention to detail has helped them build a strong reputation and gain customer trust.

3. Stay true to your values: Maina's success is rooted in their unwavering commitment to their core values of tradition, quality, and artisanal excellence. By staying true to these values, they have been able to differentiate themselves from their competitors and build a loyal customer base.

4. Family involvement: The active involvement of the Maina family in the business has been instrumental in their success. Their hands-on approach to quality control and decision-

making has allowed them to maintain a strong connection to their products and ensure that their vision is carried out.

5. Adapt to changing times: While Maina has remained committed to traditional baking methods, they have also adapted to changing consumer preferences and market trends. By introducing new products and expanding their distribution channels, they have been able to reach a wider audience without compromising on their core values.

In conclusion, the Maina family legacy is a shining example of the power of tradition, quality, and artisanal excellence. Their commitment to preserving traditional baking methods, active involvement in quality control, and adherence to their core values have set them apart from their competitors and ensured their continued success. Other companies can learn from Maina's story by embracing tradition, focusing on quality, staying true to their values, involving the family in decision-making, and adapting to changing times.

12.2 Maina's Commitment to Traditional Baking

Maina is a family-owned company that has been committed to the art of traditional baking for over a century. Founded in 1894 by the Maina family in Italy, the company has become renowned for its high-quality baked goods and its dedication to preserving traditional baking methods. Maina's success can be attributed to its unwavering commitment to maintaining the authenticity and excellence of its products.

12.2.1 Preserving Traditional Recipes and Techniques

One of the key factors behind Maina's success is its commitment to preserving traditional recipes and baking techniques. The company understands the importance of heritage and the value that traditional methods bring to their products. Maina has carefully preserved its original recipes, ensuring that each product is made with the same attention to detail and quality as it was over a century ago.

By staying true to their roots, Maina has been able to create a unique selling point in the market. Consumers appreciate the authenticity and nostalgia that comes with Maina's traditional baked goods. This commitment to tradition has allowed Maina to build a loyal customer base that values the company's dedication to preserving the art of baking.

12.2.2 Sourcing the Finest Ingredients

Maina's commitment to quality extends beyond traditional recipes and techniques. The company also places great emphasis on sourcing the finest ingredients for their products. They understand that the quality of the ingredients directly impacts the taste and overall experience of their baked goods.

Maina works closely with local farmers and suppliers to ensure that they have access to the freshest and highest-quality ingredients. By maintaining strong relationships with their suppliers, Maina can guarantee the consistency and excellence of their products. This attention to detail sets Maina apart

from its competitors and contributes to its reputation for producing exceptional baked goods.

12.2.3 Quality Control and Attention to Detail

Maina's commitment to traditional baking goes hand in hand with their dedication to quality control and attention to detail. Every step of the baking process is carefully monitored to ensure that each product meets Maina's high standards. From the selection of ingredients to the final packaging, Maina's team of skilled bakers and quality control experts meticulously oversee every aspect of production.

This commitment to quality control allows Maina to consistently deliver products that meet or exceed customer expectations. By maintaining strict quality standards, Maina has built a reputation for excellence and reliability. Customers trust Maina to provide them with consistently delicious and high-quality baked goods.

12.2.4 Innovation while Preserving Tradition

While Maina is deeply committed to preserving traditional baking methods, the company also recognizes the importance of innovation in staying relevant in a rapidly changing market. Maina has successfully found a balance between tradition and innovation, incorporating modern techniques and technologies without compromising the authenticity of their products.

Maina invests in research and development to explore new flavors, textures, and baking techniques. They continuously strive to create innovative products that appeal to evolving consumer tastes while still maintaining the essence of traditional baking. This ability to adapt and innovate has allowed Maina to expand its product range and attract new customers while retaining its loyal fan base.

12.2.5 Building a Strong Family Culture

Another crucial aspect of Maina's success is its strong family culture. The Maina family has instilled a sense of pride, passion, and dedication in every member of the company. This shared commitment to excellence and tradition creates a cohesive and motivated team that is driven to uphold Maina's values.

The Maina family actively involves themselves in the day-to-day operations of the company, ensuring that their vision and values are upheld at all times. This hands-on approach fosters a sense of unity and accountability within the organization. Employees feel a strong connection to the company and are motivated to deliver their best work.

12.2.6 Lessons for Other Companies

Maina's success offers valuable lessons for other companies, regardless of their sector or size:

1. **Preserve tradition**: Companies can benefit from preserving their heritage and staying true to their roots. Authenticity and tradition can be powerful differentiators in a competitive market.

2. **Commit to quality**: Prioritizing quality control and attention to detail is essential for

building a strong reputation and customer loyalty.

3. **Source the best ingredients**: Investing in high-quality ingredients can significantly enhance the taste and overall experience of products.

4. **Balance tradition and innovation**: Companies should find ways to innovate while still preserving the essence of their brand. Embracing new technologies and techniques can help companies stay relevant without compromising their core values.

5. **Build a strong company culture**: Fostering a sense of unity, pride, and dedication among employees can create a motivated and high-performing team.

Maina's commitment to traditional baking, quality, and family values has allowed them to thrive in a competitive market. By embracing these principles, other companies can learn from Maina's success and apply them to their own businesses.

12.3 Family Involvement in Maina's Quality Control

Maina, a renowned Italian bakery, has been able to maintain its tradition, quality, and artisanal excellence over the years. One of the key factors contributing to Maina's success is the active involvement of the family in the company's quality control processes. This section will explore how Maina's family members play a crucial role in ensuring the highest standards of quality in their products.

12.3.1 A Commitment to Excellence

Maina's commitment to excellence starts with the family's deep-rooted passion for baking. The Maina family has been involved in the bakery business for generations, and their dedication to preserving traditional baking methods is evident in every product they create. This commitment to excellence is instilled in every family member, ensuring that quality remains at the forefront of Maina's operations.

12.3.2 Hands-On Approach

One of the unique aspects of Maina's quality control is the hands-on approach taken by the family members. They actively participate in the production process, overseeing every step to ensure that the highest standards are met. From selecting the finest ingredients to monitoring the baking process, the family members are deeply involved in maintaining the quality of Maina's products.

12.3.3 Expertise and Knowledge

The Maina family's expertise and knowledge in the baking industry are invaluable when it comes to quality control. With years of experience passed down through generations, they have developed a keen understanding of the intricacies involved in creating exceptional baked goods. This expertise allows them to identify any deviations from the desired quality standards and take immediate corrective actions.

12.3.4 Training and Development

To ensure that the family members are equipped with the necessary skills and knowledge, Maina invests in continuous training and development programs. This includes both technical training related to baking techniques and quality control processes, as well as leadership and management training. By constantly improving their skills, the family members are better prepared to uphold Maina's commitment to quality.

12.3.5 Quality Control Systems

Maina has implemented robust quality control systems to maintain consistency and meet customer expectations. These systems are designed and monitored by the family members, who have an in-depth understanding of the specific requirements of each product. From raw material sourcing to packaging and distribution, every aspect of Maina's operations is carefully controlled to ensure the highest level of quality.

12.3.6 Attention to Detail

The Maina family's attention to detail is a crucial element in their quality control process. They understand that even the smallest deviation from the desired standards can impact the overall quality of their products. Therefore, they meticulously inspect every batch of baked goods, paying close attention to factors such as texture, taste, aroma, and appearance. This meticulous approach ensures that only the finest products reach the customers.

12.3.7 Customer Feedback and Continuous Improvement

Maina values customer feedback as an essential tool for continuous improvement. The family actively seeks feedback from their customers, whether through surveys, social media, or direct interactions. They carefully analyze this feedback and use it to identify areas for improvement. By incorporating customer insights into their quality control processes, Maina can adapt and evolve to meet changing consumer preferences.

12.3.8 Maintaining Tradition and Innovation

While Maina is committed to preserving traditional baking methods, they also embrace innovation to stay relevant in a competitive market. The family members play a crucial role in striking the right balance between tradition and innovation. They ensure that new techniques and technologies are implemented without compromising the core values and quality that Maina is known for.

12.3.9 Leading by Example

The family members at Maina lead by example when it comes to quality control. They set high standards for themselves and the entire team, demonstrating their unwavering commitment to excellence. This hands-on approach and dedication inspire employees at all levels to take pride in their work and strive for the highest level of quality in everything they do.

12.3.10 Lessons for Other Companies

Maina's success in maintaining quality through family involvement offers valuable lessons for other companies:

1. **Passion and Commitment**: Family businesses can benefit from instilling a deep passion and commitment to excellence in their operations.
2. **Hands-On Approach**: Actively participating in the production process allows family members to have a direct impact on quality control.
3. **Expertise and Knowledge**: Leveraging the family's expertise and knowledge in the industry can significantly contribute to maintaining high-quality standards.
4. **Continuous Training and Development**: Investing in training and development programs ensures that family members are equipped with the necessary skills to uphold quality.
5. **Robust Quality Control Systems**: Implementing effective quality control systems helps maintain consistency and meet customer expectations.
6. **Attention to Detail**: Paying attention to even the smallest details can make a significant difference in the overall quality of products.
7. **Customer Feedback and Continuous Improvement**: Actively seeking and incorporating customer feedback into quality control processes leads to continuous improvement.

8. **Balancing Tradition and Innovation**: Finding the right balance between tradition and innovation allows companies to evolve while maintaining their core values.

9. **Leading by Example**: Family members should lead by example, setting high standards and inspiring employees to strive for excellence.

By adopting these lessons, companies can enhance their quality control processes and ensure the delivery of exceptional products or services to their customers.

12.4 Lessons in Artisanal Excellence from Maina

Maina is a family-owned company that has been producing traditional baked goods for over a century. With a commitment to quality and artisanal excellence, Maina has become a renowned name in the baking industry. In this section, we will explore the lessons that other companies can learn from Maina's success in maintaining traditional baking practices while adapting to modern market demands.

12.4.1 Preserving Tradition and Craftsmanship

One of the key lessons that companies can learn from Maina is the importance of preserving tradition and craftsmanship. Maina has stayed true to its roots by using traditional baking methods and recipes that have been passed down through generations. This commitment to preserving the art of baking has allowed Maina to create products that are not only delicious but also carry a sense of heritage and authenticity.

By embracing tradition and craftsmanship, companies can differentiate themselves in a market that is often dominated by mass-produced goods. Whether it is in the food industry or any other sector, maintaining a connection to the past and honoring the skills and techniques of previous generations can create a unique selling point and attract customers who value quality and authenticity.

12.4.2 Attention to Ingredients and Sourcing

Another lesson that companies can learn from Maina is the importance of attention to ingredients and sourcing. Maina prides itself on using only the finest ingredients, sourced from trusted suppliers. This commitment to quality ensures that every product that leaves their bakery meets the highest standards.

By prioritizing the quality of ingredients and carefully selecting suppliers, companies can enhance the overall quality of their products or services. Customers today are increasingly conscious of what they consume and are willing to pay a premium for products that are made with high-quality ingredients. By focusing on sourcing and using the best materials available, companies can build a reputation for excellence and attract discerning customers.

12.4.3 Continuous Improvement and Innovation

While Maina is deeply rooted in tradition, they also understand the importance of continuous improvement and innovation. They have embraced

modern technology and techniques to streamline their production processes and ensure consistency in their products. By combining traditional methods with modern advancements, Maina has been able to meet the demands of a changing market while maintaining the quality and taste that customers expect.

Companies can learn from Maina's approach by embracing innovation and continuously seeking ways to improve their products or services. This can involve investing in research and development, adopting new technologies, or exploring creative solutions to meet customer needs. By staying ahead of the curve and constantly evolving, companies can remain competitive and relevant in a rapidly changing business landscape.

12.4.4 Building Strong Relationships with Customers

Maina has built a strong and loyal customer base by prioritizing customer satisfaction. They have fostered a sense of community and connection with their customers, creating a brand that is trusted and respected. Maina understands the importance of listening to their customers' feedback and incorporating it into their business practices.

Companies can learn from Maina's customer-centric approach by actively engaging with their customers and building strong relationships. By understanding their customers' needs and preferences, companies can tailor their products or services to better meet those demands. This not only enhances customer satisfaction but also fosters loyalty and advocacy, leading to long-term success.

12.4.5 Balancing Tradition and Adaptability

Maina has successfully balanced tradition and adaptability, allowing them to stay relevant in a rapidly changing market. While they have maintained their commitment to traditional baking practices, they have also embraced new trends and consumer preferences. This ability to adapt and evolve has allowed Maina to expand their product range and cater to a wider audience.

Companies can learn from Maina's approach by finding the right balance between tradition and adaptability. It is essential to honor the core values and heritage of the company while also being open to change and innovation. By staying true to their roots while embracing new opportunities, companies can navigate the challenges of a dynamic business environment and ensure long-term success.

In conclusion, Maina's success in artisanal excellence offers valuable lessons for companies across industries. By preserving tradition and craftsmanship, paying attention to ingredients and sourcing, embracing continuous improvement and innovation, building strong customer relationships, and balancing tradition with adaptability, companies can learn from Maina's example and achieve their own success in their respective fields.

Kaiser

13.1 The Kaiser Family Story

The Kaiser Family Story is a testament to the power of innovation and expansion in the food industry. The Kaiser family, led by patriarch John Kaiser, started their journey in the early 1950s with a small butcher shop in a suburban neighborhood. Over the years, they transformed their business into a thriving food production company that is now known for its high-quality products and commitment to customer satisfaction.

13.1.1 From Humble Beginnings

The Kaiser family's journey began with a simple vision: to provide their community with fresh and delicious food. John Kaiser, a skilled butcher, opened a small shop where he personally sourced and prepared the meat for his customers. His dedication to quality and his passion for serving his community quickly gained him a loyal customer base.

As the demand for their products grew, the Kaiser family realized the need to expand their operations. They invested in state-of-the-art equipment and hired a team of skilled professionals to help them meet the increasing demand. This expansion allowed them to not only serve their local community but also reach a wider market.

13.1.2 Innovation in Food Production

One of the key factors that set the Kaiser family apart from their competitors was their commitment to innovation in food production. They constantly

sought new ways to improve their processes and create unique products that would delight their customers.

The Kaiser family invested in research and development, exploring new technologies and techniques to enhance the quality and taste of their products. They also focused on sustainability, implementing eco-friendly practices in their production processes. This commitment to innovation and sustainability not only helped them stay ahead of the competition but also resonated with their customers who valued these principles.

13.1.3 Family Values in Kaiser's Business Strategy

Family values have always been at the core of the Kaiser family's business strategy. They believe in fostering a strong sense of unity, trust, and loyalty among their employees. The family actively encourages open communication and collaboration, creating a supportive work environment where everyone feels valued and motivated.

The Kaiser family also places a strong emphasis on maintaining strong relationships with their suppliers and partners. They believe in treating them as an extension of their family, fostering long-term partnerships based on trust and mutual respect. This approach has allowed them to build a reliable supply chain and ensure the consistent quality of their products.

13.1.4 Applying Kaiser's Expansion Strategies to Other Companies

The Kaiser family's success in the food industry holds valuable lessons for other companies looking to expand and innovate. Here are some key takeaways:

1. **Customer-Centric Approach**: The Kaiser family's commitment to customer satisfaction has been instrumental in their success. They prioritize understanding their customers' needs and preferences, and constantly strive to exceed their expectations. Other companies can learn from this by placing the customer at the center of their business strategy.

2. **Investment in Innovation**: The Kaiser family's dedication to innovation has allowed them to stay ahead of the curve and continuously improve their products and processes. Companies in any industry can benefit from investing in research and development to drive innovation and maintain a competitive edge.

3. **Strong Company Culture**: The Kaiser family's focus on fostering a strong company culture based on family values has created a positive and motivated workforce. Other companies can learn from this by prioritizing employee well-being, open communication, and collaboration.

4. **Building Strong Partnerships**: The Kaiser family's approach to building strong

relationships with suppliers and partners has been crucial to their success. Companies can benefit from nurturing long-term partnerships based on trust and mutual respect, which can contribute to a reliable supply chain and consistent product quality.

5. **Sustainability and Responsibility**: The Kaiser family's commitment to sustainability and responsible business practices has resonated with their customers. Companies can learn from this by incorporating sustainable practices into their operations and aligning their values with those of their target market.

In conclusion, the Kaiser family's story exemplifies the power of innovation and expansion in the food industry. Their commitment to quality, customer satisfaction, and family values has been the driving force behind their success. By applying their expansion strategies and embracing their core values, other companies can learn valuable lessons and achieve their own success in their respective industries.

13.2 Kaiser's Innovation in Food Production

Kaiser is a family-owned company that has made significant strides in the food industry through its innovative approach to food production. With a rich history and a commitment to quality, Kaiser has become a prominent player in the market. In this section, we will explore Kaiser's innovation in food production and the family values that have contributed to its success.

13.2.1 A Legacy of Quality and Tradition

Kaiser's journey in the food industry began several decades ago when the family patriarch, John Kaiser, started a small bakery in his hometown. From the very beginning, the company focused on delivering high-quality products that were made with traditional recipes and techniques. This commitment to quality has been passed down through the generations and remains a cornerstone of Kaiser's success.

13.2.2 Embracing Innovation in Food Production

One of the key factors that sets Kaiser apart from its competitors is its continuous focus on innovation in food production. The company has invested heavily in research and development to stay ahead of the curve and meet the evolving needs of consumers. Kaiser has embraced new technologies and processes to improve efficiency, enhance product quality, and reduce environmental impact.

For example, Kaiser has implemented advanced automation systems in its production facilities to streamline operations and ensure consistency in product quality. These systems have not only increased productivity but also allowed the company to maintain high standards of food safety and hygiene.

Furthermore, Kaiser has been at the forefront of sustainable food production practices. The company has implemented eco-friendly initiatives such as reducing water and energy consumption, optimizing packaging materials, and sourcing ingredients from sustainable suppliers. By prioritizing sustainability,

Kaiser has not only reduced its environmental footprint but also appealed to a growing segment of environmentally conscious consumers.

13.2.3 Family Values Driving Success

Family values play a crucial role in Kaiser's business strategy and have been instrumental in its success. The Kaiser family has instilled a strong sense of unity, trust, and loyalty within the company, creating a supportive and collaborative work environment. This familial atmosphere has fostered a deep commitment to the company's mission and values among employees, resulting in a highly motivated workforce.

Moreover, the family's long-term vision and dedication to the company's success have allowed Kaiser to make strategic decisions that prioritize sustainable growth over short-term gains. This approach has enabled the company to invest in research and development, expand its production capabilities, and enter new markets.

13.2.4 Applying Kaiser's Expansion Strategies to Other Companies

While every company is unique, there are valuable lessons that other businesses can learn from Kaiser's success in food production and expansion. Here are some key takeaways:

1. **Invest in Research and Development**: By allocating resources to research and development, companies can stay ahead of the competition and meet the changing needs of consumers. Innovation should be a

continuous process to drive growth and maintain relevance in the market.

2. **Embrace Technology**: Companies should embrace technological advancements to improve efficiency, enhance product quality, and reduce environmental impact. Automation and digitalization can streamline operations and provide a competitive edge.

3. **Prioritize Sustainability**: Consumers are increasingly conscious of the environmental impact of their choices. By adopting sustainable practices, companies can attract a growing segment of environmentally conscious consumers and differentiate themselves in the market.

4. **Foster a Strong Company Culture**: Building a strong company culture based on trust, unity, and loyalty can create a motivated and engaged workforce. This, in turn, drives productivity, innovation, and long-term success.

5. **Have a Long-Term Vision**: Companies should prioritize sustainable growth over short-term gains. Having a long-term vision allows for strategic decision-making and investment in areas such as research and development, production capabilities, and market expansion.

In conclusion, Kaiser's innovation in food production, coupled with its commitment to quality and family values, has been instrumental in its success. By embracing technology, prioritizing sustainability, fostering a strong company culture, and having a long-term vision, other companies can learn valuable lessons from Kaiser's expansion strategies.

13.3 Family Values in Kaiser's Business Strategy

Family values play a crucial role in the success of any family-owned business, and Kaiser is no exception. As a prominent player in the food industry, Kaiser has demonstrated how incorporating strong family values into their business strategy can lead to innovation and expansion. By understanding and embracing these values, other companies can learn valuable lessons and apply them to their own growth and development.

13.3.1 A Strong Sense of Unity and Purpose

One of the key family values that Kaiser embodies is a strong sense of unity and purpose. The Kaiser family understands the importance of working together towards a common goal. This unity is not only limited to family members but extends to all employees within the organization. By fostering a sense of belonging and shared purpose, Kaiser has created a work environment that is conducive to collaboration and innovation.

13.3.2 Long-Term Vision and Commitment

Family-owned businesses often have the advantage of taking a long-term view of their operations, and Kaiser is no different. The Kaiser family has shown a

deep commitment to the company's growth and success over generations. This long-term vision allows them to make strategic decisions that may not yield immediate results but contribute to the sustainable growth of the business in the long run. Other companies can learn from Kaiser's commitment to their core values and their ability to make decisions that align with their long-term vision.

13.3.3 Trust and Empowerment

Trust is a fundamental aspect of any successful family business, and Kaiser understands its significance. The Kaiser family has built a culture of trust within the organization, empowering employees to take ownership of their work and make decisions that contribute to the company's success. This trust extends to their relationships with suppliers, customers, and other stakeholders, fostering strong partnerships and collaboration. By trusting their employees and stakeholders, Kaiser has created an environment that encourages innovation and fosters loyalty.

13.3.4 Ethical and Responsible Practices

Kaiser places a strong emphasis on ethical and responsible business practices. The family values of integrity, honesty, and transparency are deeply ingrained in the company's culture. Kaiser ensures that their products are of the highest quality and sourced responsibly, taking into consideration the impact on the environment and the well-being of their customers. By prioritizing ethical practices, Kaiser has gained the trust and loyalty of their

customers, setting them apart from their competitors.

13.3.5 Nurturing Relationships

Family-owned businesses often excel in building and nurturing relationships, and Kaiser is no exception. The Kaiser family understands the importance of fostering strong relationships with their employees, customers, and suppliers. They prioritize open communication, actively listen to feedback, and value the contributions of all stakeholders. By nurturing these relationships, Kaiser has created a loyal customer base and a network of trusted partners, enabling them to expand their business and explore new opportunities.

13.3.6 Embracing Innovation

Innovation is a key driver of success in any industry, and Kaiser recognizes its importance. The Kaiser family encourages a culture of innovation within the organization, empowering employees to think creatively and explore new ideas. They invest in research and development, constantly seeking ways to improve their products and processes. By embracing innovation, Kaiser has been able to stay ahead of the competition and adapt to changing market trends.

13.3.7 Balancing Tradition and Adaptability

Kaiser has successfully managed to strike a balance between tradition and adaptability. While they hold onto their core values and traditions, they also recognize the need to adapt to evolving customer preferences and market dynamics. This ability to

embrace change while staying true to their roots has allowed Kaiser to remain relevant and competitive in the food industry. Other companies can learn from Kaiser's approach to balancing tradition and adaptability, ensuring they stay connected to their heritage while embracing innovation.

13.3.8 Investing in Employee Development

Kaiser understands the importance of investing in their employees' development and growth. They provide training and development opportunities, empowering their workforce to reach their full potential. By nurturing their employees' skills and talents, Kaiser has built a team of dedicated professionals who are committed to the company's success. This investment in employee development not only enhances the company's capabilities but also fosters a sense of loyalty and commitment among the workforce.

13.3.9 Giving Back to the Community

Family-owned businesses often have a strong sense of social responsibility, and Kaiser is no different. The Kaiser family believes in giving back to the community and making a positive impact. They actively engage in philanthropic initiatives, supporting local communities and charitable organizations. By demonstrating their commitment to social responsibility, Kaiser has built a positive reputation and strengthened their relationships with the community.

13.3.10 Lessons for Other Companies

Other companies can learn valuable lessons from Kaiser's success. By incorporating family values into their business strategy, companies can foster unity, trust, and a sense of purpose among their employees. They can also take a long-term view, make ethical and responsible decisions, and invest in employee development. Balancing tradition and adaptability, embracing innovation, and giving back to the community are also key lessons that can contribute to the success of any organization.

In conclusion, Kaiser's success in the food industry can be attributed to their strong adherence to family values. By embracing unity, trust, long-term vision, and ethical practices, Kaiser has been able to innovate and expand their business. Other companies can learn from Kaiser's approach and apply these lessons to their own strategies, regardless of their sector, size, or leadership. Incorporating family values into the business strategy can lead to sustainable growth, loyal customers, and a positive impact on the community.

13.4 Applying Kaiser's Expansion Strategies to Other Companies

Kaiser, a successful family company in the food industry, has demonstrated remarkable innovation and expansion strategies that can serve as valuable lessons for other companies looking to grow and thrive. With their unique approach to food production and strong emphasis on family values, Kaiser has managed to establish itself as a leader in the industry. In this section, we will explore the key expansion strategies employed by Kaiser and how they can be applied to other companies.

13.4.1 Embrace Innovation and Adaptability

One of the primary reasons for Kaiser's success in the food industry is their unwavering commitment to innovation and adaptability. They have consistently embraced new technologies and processes to improve their food production methods and stay ahead of the competition. By investing in research and development, Kaiser has been able to introduce new products and expand their offerings to cater to changing consumer demands.

Other companies can learn from Kaiser's approach by fostering a culture of innovation within their organizations. Encouraging employees to think creatively and explore new ideas can lead to breakthrough innovations and help companies stay relevant in a rapidly evolving market. Additionally, companies should be open to adopting new technologies and processes that can enhance their operations and improve efficiency.

13.4.2 Focus on Quality and Customer Satisfaction

Kaiser has built a strong reputation for delivering high-quality food products that meet the expectations of their customers. They prioritize quality control at every stage of the production process, ensuring that their products are consistently of the highest standard. By maintaining a strong focus on quality, Kaiser has been able to establish trust and loyalty among their customer base.

Other companies can learn from Kaiser's emphasis on quality by prioritizing customer satisfaction and consistently delivering products or services that meet or exceed customer expectations. By investing in quality control measures and continuously improving their offerings, companies can build a strong brand reputation and foster customer loyalty.

13.4.3 Establish Strategic Partnerships

Kaiser has successfully expanded its reach and market presence through strategic partnerships with other companies in the food industry. By collaborating with suppliers, distributors, and retailers, Kaiser has been able to extend its distribution network and reach a wider customer base. These partnerships have allowed Kaiser to tap into new markets and increase their market share.

Other companies can learn from Kaiser's approach by actively seeking out strategic partnerships that can help them expand their reach and access new markets. By leveraging the strengths and resources of their partners, companies can accelerate their growth and achieve greater success.

13.4.4 Invest in Branding and Marketing

Kaiser has invested heavily in branding and marketing to create a strong brand identity and increase brand awareness. They have effectively communicated their values, mission, and commitment to quality through various marketing channels, including advertising campaigns, social media, and packaging design. This has helped Kaiser differentiate itself from competitors and build a loyal customer base.

Other companies can learn from Kaiser's branding and marketing strategies by investing in building a strong brand identity and effectively communicating their unique value proposition to customers. By developing a compelling brand story and utilizing various marketing channels, companies can increase their visibility and attract a larger customer base.

13.4.5 Foster a Strong Company Culture

Kaiser places a strong emphasis on family values and has fostered a company culture that promotes teamwork, collaboration, and mutual respect. They prioritize the well-being and development of their employees, recognizing that a motivated and engaged workforce is crucial for success. This strong company culture has contributed to Kaiser's ability to attract and retain top talent.

Other companies can learn from Kaiser's focus on company culture by creating a positive and inclusive work environment that values and supports employees. By fostering a culture of trust, transparency, and continuous learning, companies can enhance employee satisfaction, productivity, and overall business performance.

13.4.6 Expand Geographically

Kaiser's expansion strategies have also included geographical expansion, allowing them to tap into new markets and diversify their customer base. By carefully analyzing market opportunities and adapting their products to suit local preferences, Kaiser has successfully expanded its operations beyond its initial market.

Other companies can learn from Kaiser's geographical expansion by conducting thorough market research and identifying potential opportunities in new regions. By tailoring their products or services to meet the specific needs and preferences of different markets, companies can successfully expand their operations and capture new customers.

In conclusion, Kaiser's success in the food industry can be attributed to their innovative mindset, focus on quality, strategic partnerships, branding and marketing efforts, strong company culture, and geographical expansion. By applying these strategies, other companies can learn valuable lessons and increase their chances of achieving sustainable growth and success.

Esselunga

14.1 The Esselunga Family Legacy

Esselunga is a renowned Italian supermarket chain that has achieved remarkable success in the retail industry. Founded in 1957 by Bernardo Caprotti, Esselunga has grown to become one of the largest and most respected supermarket chains in Italy. The company's commitment to customer focus and its strong family legacy have played a significant role in its success.

14.1.1 The Founding of Esselunga

The Esselunga story began when Bernardo Caprotti, a visionary entrepreneur, opened the first store in Milan. Caprotti's aim was to create a supermarket that would revolutionize the shopping experience for Italian consumers. He focused on providing a wide range of high-quality products at affordable prices, combined with exceptional customer service.

14.1.2 The Family's Commitment to Excellence

From the very beginning, the Caprotti family instilled a culture of excellence within Esselunga. They emphasized the importance of delivering the highest standards of quality in every aspect of the business. This commitment to excellence has been a driving force behind Esselunga's success and has helped the company build a strong reputation for reliability and trustworthiness.

14.1.3 Customer-Centric Approach

One of the key factors that set Esselunga apart from its competitors is its unwavering focus on the customer. The company has always prioritized understanding and meeting the needs of its customers. Esselunga invests heavily in market research and customer feedback to ensure that it can provide the best possible shopping experience. This customer-centric approach has allowed the company to build long-lasting relationships with its customers and create a loyal customer base.

14.1.4 Innovation and Adaptability

Esselunga has consistently embraced innovation and adapted to changing market trends. The company has been quick to adopt new technologies and implement innovative solutions to enhance the shopping experience. For example, Esselunga was one of the first supermarket chains in Italy to introduce self-checkout systems, which streamlined the payment process for customers. This willingness to embrace change and stay ahead of the curve has been instrumental in Esselunga's continued success.

14.1.5 Family Involvement and Leadership

The Caprotti family's active involvement in Esselunga's operations has been a crucial factor in the company's success. The family has maintained a strong presence in the business, with family members holding key leadership positions. This continuity in leadership has allowed Esselunga to maintain its core values and long-term vision, ensuring the company's sustained growth and success.

14.1.6 Employee Engagement and Development

Esselunga recognizes the importance of its employees in delivering exceptional customer service. The company places a strong emphasis on employee engagement and development, providing extensive training programs and opportunities for career growth. Esselunga believes that motivated and well-trained employees are essential for creating a positive shopping experience for customers. This focus on employee satisfaction has resulted in a dedicated and passionate workforce, contributing to the company's overall success.

14.1.7 Community Involvement and Social Responsibility

Esselunga is deeply committed to giving back to the communities it serves. The company actively engages in various social responsibility initiatives, supporting local charities, and promoting sustainable practices. Esselunga's commitment to social responsibility has not only had a positive impact on the communities it operates in but has also enhanced its brand reputation and customer loyalty.

14.1.8 Key Takeaways from Esselunga's Success

Esselunga's success can be attributed to several key factors:

1. **Customer Focus**: Prioritizing the needs and preferences of customers and consistently

delivering an exceptional shopping experience.

2. **Commitment to Excellence**: Maintaining high standards of quality in all aspects of the business.
3. **Innovation and Adaptability**: Embracing new technologies and staying ahead of market trends.
4. **Family Involvement**: Maintaining a strong family presence in the business and ensuring continuity in leadership.
5. **Employee Engagement**: Investing in employee training and development to create a motivated and dedicated workforce.
6. **Community Involvement**: Engaging in social responsibility initiatives and giving back to the communities it serves.

Other companies can learn from Esselunga's success by prioritizing customer satisfaction, fostering a culture of excellence, embracing innovation, and involving the family in business operations. Additionally, investing in employee development and engaging in social responsibility initiatives can contribute to long-term success and a positive brand image. Esselunga's story serves as an inspiration for companies across industries, showcasing the power of family values and a customer-centric approach in achieving sustainable growth and success.

14.2 Esselunga's Customer-Centric Approach

Esselunga, a prominent Italian supermarket chain, has achieved remarkable success by adopting a customer-centric approach in its business strategy.

This chapter explores how Esselunga's commitment to customer satisfaction has propelled its growth and provides valuable insights for other companies looking to enhance their customer focus.

14.2.1 A Legacy of Customer Service

Esselunga's customer-centric approach can be traced back to its founder, Bernardo Caprotti. From the inception of the company in 1957, Caprotti emphasized the importance of providing exceptional service to customers. He believed that by understanding and meeting the needs of customers, a company could build long-term loyalty and success.

14.2.2 Creating a Unique Shopping Experience

One of the key aspects of Esselunga's customer-centric approach is its commitment to creating a unique shopping experience. The company invests heavily in store design, layout, and ambiance to ensure that customers feel comfortable and enjoy their time in the supermarket. Esselunga stores are known for their spaciousness, cleanliness, and attractive displays, which contribute to a pleasant shopping environment.

14.2.3 Personalized Customer Service

Esselunga goes above and beyond to provide personalized customer service. The company trains its employees to be knowledgeable about the products and services offered, enabling them to assist customers effectively. Esselunga staff members are known for their friendly and helpful attitude, creating a welcoming atmosphere for shoppers. Additionally, the company offers personalized loyalty programs and tailored promotions to cater to individual customer preferences.

14.2.4 Quality Products and Competitive Pricing

Esselunga's commitment to customer satisfaction extends to the quality of its products. The company carefully selects its suppliers and rigorously tests the products to ensure they meet high standards. By offering a wide range of high-quality products, Esselunga builds trust with its customers, who rely on the supermarket for their everyday needs.

In addition to quality, Esselunga is also known for its competitive pricing. The company strives to offer affordable prices without compromising on product quality. This combination of quality and value has been instrumental in attracting and retaining customers.

14.2.5 Innovation and Technology

Esselunga recognizes the importance of embracing innovation and technology to enhance the customer experience. The company has invested in various technological solutions, such as self-checkout systems and mobile apps, to streamline the shopping process and provide convenience to customers. Esselunga also utilizes data analytics to gain insights into customer preferences and tailor its offerings accordingly.

14.2.6 Community Engagement and Social Responsibility

Another aspect of Esselunga's customer-centric approach is its commitment to community engagement and social responsibility. The company actively supports local initiatives and charities, demonstrating its dedication to giving back to the communities it serves. By aligning its values with those of its customers, Esselunga strengthens its relationship with the community and fosters a sense of loyalty.

14.2.7 Continuous Improvement and Feedback

Esselunga understands the importance of continuous improvement and actively seeks feedback from its customers. The company encourages customers to provide suggestions and opinions through various channels, such as surveys and online platforms. By listening to customer feedback and implementing necessary changes, Esselunga demonstrates its commitment to meeting customer expectations and staying ahead of the competition.

14.2.8 Lessons for Other Companies

Esselunga's customer-centric approach offers valuable lessons for other companies seeking to enhance their customer focus:

1. Prioritize customer satisfaction: Make customer satisfaction a top priority and align all aspects of your business strategy to meet their needs.

2. Create a unique experience: Invest in creating a unique and enjoyable experience for customers, whether it's through store design, ambiance, or personalized services.

3. Provide personalized customer service: Train your employees to provide personalized and knowledgeable customer service, ensuring that customers feel valued and supported.

4. Focus on product quality and competitive pricing: Offer high-quality products at competitive prices to build trust and loyalty with customers.

5. Embrace innovation and technology: Utilize innovative solutions and technology to enhance the customer experience and streamline processes.

6. Engage with the community: Demonstrate social responsibility and engage with the local community to build a positive brand image and foster customer loyalty.

7. Seek continuous improvement: Actively seek feedback from customers and implement necessary changes to continuously improve and meet evolving customer expectations.

By adopting these principles and incorporating a customer-centric approach into their strategies, companies can cultivate strong customer relationships, drive growth, and achieve long-term success. Esselunga's success story serves as a testament to the power of putting customers at the center of business operations.

14.3 Family Involvement in Esselunga's Retail Strategy

Family involvement plays a crucial role in the success of Esselunga, one of Italy's largest supermarket chains. Founded in 1957 by Bernardo Caprotti, Esselunga has grown to become a household name, known for its customer-centric approach and commitment to quality. The Caprotti family's active participation in the company's retail strategy has been instrumental in shaping Esselunga's growth and maintaining its competitive edge in the market.

14.3.1 A Family Legacy of Retail Expertise

The Caprotti family's deep understanding of the retail industry has been passed down through generations, forming the foundation of Esselunga's success. Bernardo Caprotti, the company's founder, had a rich background in the retail sector, having worked in his family's grocery store from a young age. This experience instilled in him a strong work ethic and a keen eye for customer needs.

Bernardo Caprotti's son, Giuseppe Caprotti, continued his father's legacy by joining Esselunga and eventually taking over as CEO. Giuseppe's extensive knowledge of the retail industry, combined with his innovative thinking, allowed him to steer Esselunga towards continuous growth and expansion. Today, the third generation of the Caprotti family, led by Giuseppe's son, Violetta Caprotti, remains actively involved in the company's operations, ensuring the preservation of Esselunga's core values.

14.3.2 A Customer-Centric Approach

Esselunga's retail strategy revolves around putting the customer at the center of everything they do. The Caprotti family's involvement in the company allows them to have a deep understanding of their customers' needs and preferences. This insight enables them to make informed decisions that align with their target market's demands.

The family's hands-on approach extends to every aspect of Esselunga's operations. They actively engage with customers, seeking feedback and suggestions to improve their shopping experience. This direct interaction helps them stay connected to their customer base and build long-lasting relationships.

Furthermore, the Caprotti family's commitment to quality is evident in Esselunga's product selection. They prioritize offering a wide range of high-quality products, including fresh produce, organic options, and gourmet items. This dedication to quality has earned Esselunga a reputation as a trusted retailer, further strengthening customer loyalty.

14.3.3 Innovation and Adaptability

Esselunga's success can also be attributed to its ability to innovate and adapt to changing market trends. The Caprotti family's involvement allows them to stay agile and make swift decisions when necessary. They closely monitor industry developments and consumer behavior, enabling them to introduce new products and services that meet evolving customer demands.

For example, Esselunga was one of the first supermarket chains in Italy to introduce self-checkout systems, providing customers with a convenient and efficient shopping experience. They have also embraced e-commerce, offering online shopping and home delivery services to cater to the growing demand for digital convenience.

The family's involvement in Esselunga's retail strategy ensures that the company remains at the forefront of innovation, constantly exploring new ways to enhance the customer experience and stay ahead of competitors.

14.3.4 Maintaining a Strong Company Culture

Family involvement in Esselunga's retail strategy goes beyond decision-making and innovation. The Caprotti family plays a vital role in maintaining a strong company culture that fosters employee satisfaction and loyalty. They prioritize creating a positive work environment, valuing their employees' contributions, and providing opportunities for growth and development.

The family's hands-on approach extends to their interactions with employees, fostering a sense of unity and shared purpose. They actively engage with staff members, listen to their ideas, and recognize their achievements. This inclusive and supportive culture has resulted in a highly motivated workforce that is committed to delivering exceptional customer service.

14.3.5 Lessons for Other Companies

Esselunga's success story offers valuable lessons for other companies, regardless of their sector, size, or leadership structure. Here are some key takeaways:

1. **Customer-Centric Approach**: Prioritize understanding and meeting customer needs to build strong relationships and foster loyalty.

2. **Family Involvement**: Actively involve family members in decision-making processes to leverage their industry expertise and maintain a long-term vision.

3. **Innovation and Adaptability**: Stay agile and embrace innovation to meet changing market trends and consumer demands.

4. **Maintain a Strong Company Culture**: Foster a positive work environment that values employees' contributions, encourages growth, and promotes a sense of unity.

By incorporating these principles into their own strategies, companies can enhance their competitiveness, strengthen customer relationships, and drive long-term success.

Esselunga's journey exemplifies the power of family involvement in shaping a company's retail strategy. The Caprotti family's deep understanding of the industry, customer-centric approach, and commitment to innovation have propelled Esselunga to become a leading player in the supermarket sector. Their story serves as an inspiration for businesses seeking to thrive in a competitive market by embracing family values and leveraging their unique strengths.

14.4 Key Takeaways from Esselunga's Success

Esselunga, a family-owned retail company based in Italy, has achieved remarkable success in the highly competitive grocery industry. With a focus on customer satisfaction and a commitment to quality, Esselunga has become a household name in Italy. In this section, we will explore the key takeaways from Esselunga's success and what other companies can learn from their approach.

14.4.1 Customer-Centric Approach

One of the main reasons behind Esselunga's success is their unwavering commitment to customer satisfaction. They have built a reputation for providing exceptional customer service and going above and beyond to meet their customers' needs. Esselunga understands that happy customers are loyal customers, and they have made it a priority to create a positive shopping experience for every individual who walks through their doors.

Other companies can learn from Esselunga's customer-centric approach by prioritizing customer satisfaction and making it a core value of their business. By understanding and meeting the needs of their customers, companies can build strong relationships and foster loyalty, leading to long-term success.

14.4.2 Emphasis on Quality

Esselunga has always placed a strong emphasis on quality in all aspects of their business. From the products they offer to the service they provide, Esselunga ensures that every aspect of their operations meets the highest standards. They carefully select their suppliers, focusing on quality and sustainability, and rigorously test their products to guarantee their customers' satisfaction.

Other companies can learn from Esselunga's commitment to quality by prioritizing excellence in their own products and services. By consistently delivering high-quality offerings, companies can build trust with their customers and differentiate themselves from competitors.

14.4.3 Innovation and Adaptability

Esselunga understands the importance of staying ahead of the curve in a rapidly changing market. They have embraced innovation and adapted their business model to meet evolving customer demands. From introducing new technologies in their stores to implementing efficient supply chain management systems, Esselunga has continuously sought ways to improve their operations and enhance the customer experience.

Other companies can learn from Esselunga's approach to innovation and adaptability by embracing change and proactively seeking opportunities for improvement. By staying agile and open to new ideas, companies can stay competitive and thrive in an ever-changing business landscape.

14.4.4 Strong Family Involvement

As a family-owned company, Esselunga benefits from the strong involvement of the Caprotti family, who founded and continues to lead the organization. The family's long-term vision, commitment to the company's values, and hands-on approach have played a crucial role in Esselunga's success. The Caprotti family has instilled a sense of pride and ownership in their employees, creating a strong company culture that drives performance and fosters loyalty.

Other companies can learn from Esselunga's family involvement by recognizing the value of leadership continuity and the importance of aligning the family's values with the company's mission. By nurturing a strong company culture and fostering a sense of purpose, companies can inspire their employees and drive success.

14.4.5 Community Engagement and Social Responsibility

Esselunga has always been deeply committed to the communities they serve. They actively engage with local organizations, support charitable initiatives, and promote sustainable practices. By giving back to the community and prioritizing social responsibility, Esselunga has built a positive brand image and earned the trust and loyalty of their customers.

Other companies can learn from Esselunga's community engagement and social responsibility by recognizing the importance of being a responsible corporate citizen. By actively contributing to the well-being of the communities they operate in, companies can build strong relationships and enhance their reputation.

14.4.6 Continuous Improvement and Learning

Esselunga's success can also be attributed to their commitment to continuous improvement and learning. They regularly gather feedback from their customers and employees, analyze market trends, and invest in employee training and development. By constantly seeking ways to improve and staying ahead of the competition, Esselunga has been able to maintain their position as a market leader.

Other companies can learn from Esselunga's focus on continuous improvement by fostering a culture of learning and innovation within their organizations. By encouraging employees to embrace change, take risks, and continuously develop their skills, companies can drive growth and stay ahead in a rapidly evolving business environment.

In conclusion, Esselunga's success can be attributed to their customer-centric approach, emphasis on quality, innovation and adaptability, strong family involvement, community engagement, and commitment to continuous improvement. By learning from Esselunga's strategies and incorporating these key takeaways into their own business models, companies in any industry can increase their chances of achieving long-term success.

Unleashing Power - A Symphony of Success

As we draw the final curtain on our exploration of "Power: The Secrets of 13 Successful Family Companies," we find ourselves immersed in the symphony of triumphs, philosophies, and invaluable lessons echoed by these extraordinary enterprises. Each company, a unique instrument in this grand orchestra of success, has shared its melody, contributing to the harmonious blend of family-driven accomplishments.

From the ingenuity of IKEA to the precision of Toyota, the sweetness of Ferrero to the adventurous spirit of Patagonia, and the resilience of Volkswagen to the culinary finesse of Rana, we've traversed a diverse landscape of industries, sizes, and leadership styles. Benetton, Zanussi, Diesel, Luxottica, Maina, Kaiser, and Esselunga each brought a distinct note to this symphony, showcasing the limitless possibilities woven into the fabric of family businesses.

Their collective secret lies not in a single formula but in the orchestration of timeless principles: unwavering commitment to core values, visionary leadership, adaptability to change, and a deep-seated sense of familial identity. These companies, hailing from different sectors and scales, illuminate the truth that success is not confined to a specific blueprint; rather, it emerges from the dynamic interplay of passion, resilience, and a commitment to lasting legacies.

What can other companies glean from these luminaries? The answer resonates in the pages that precede this closing. Embrace innovation like Diesel, nurture sustainability like Patagonia, cultivate a resilient family culture like Ferrero, and remain agile in the face of challenges like Maina. The lessons are diverse, yet the underlying theme is universal: family values, when woven into the fabric of business, become a source of enduring strength.

As we bid farewell to this journey, let the insights garnered from IKEA's vision, Toyota's precision, and Esselunga's commitment linger in your entrepreneurial spirit. May the stories shared inspire a new generation of businesses to harness the power within their familial bonds, to rise above challenges, and to craft their own symphony of success.

In the end, "Power" is not just a title; it's a testament to the indomitable force that family-driven enterprises bring to the global stage. The secrets are unveiled, the melodies shared, and the stage is set for a new era of businesses fueled by the enduring power of family.

Summary

Preface 3

An Intimate Odyssey.. 3

Exploring the DNA of Success 3

Secrets Unveiled, Lessons Learned........................ 3

A Blueprint for Success...................................... 4

Beyond the Pages... 4

Introduction.. 5

1.1 Understanding Family Companies..................... 5

1.2 The Importance of Family Values 9

1.2.1 Defining Family Values 10

1.2.2 Alignment with Stakeholders.....................10

1.2.3 Continuity and Stability 11

1.2.4 Ethical Decision-Making............................11

1.2.5 Flexibility and Adaptability........................12

1.2.6 Lessons for Other Companies.....................12

1.3 The Unique Challenges of Family Companies
....14

1.3.1 Balancing Family and Business Dynamics
....14

1.3.2 Succession Planning and Leadership
Transition..15

1.3.3 Maintaining a Long-Term Perspective....15

1.3.4 Professionalizing the Business 16

1.3.5 Nurturing Family Values and Culture 16

1.3.6 Building Trust and Reputation 17

1.4 The Success Stories of Family Companies 18

1.4.1 IKEA: Building a Global Empire.................. 18

1.4.2 Toyota: The Power of Continuous Improvement................. 19

1.4.3 Ferrero: Innovation and Tradition........... 19

1.4.4 Patagonia: Environmental Responsibility and Ethical Leadership 19

1.4.5 Volkswagen: Navigating Challenges and Rebuilding Trust 20

1.4.6 Rana: From Small Business to Pasta Empire... 20

1.4.7 Benetton: Fashion, Diversity, and Social Impact 21

1.4.8 Zanussi: Innovation and Adaptability in the Home Appliance Industry 21

1.4.9 Diesel: Creativity, Rebellion, and Brand Identity 21

1.4.10 Luxottica: Eyewear Dominance and Vertical Integration.................................. 22

1.4.11 Maina: Tradition, Quality, and Artisanal Excellence 22

1.4.12 Kaiser: Innovation and Expansion in the Food Industry... 23

1.4.13 Esselunga: Customer Focus and Retail Success... 23

IKEA... 25

2.1 The History and Origins of IKEA 25

2.2 The IKEA Business Model 29

2.2.1 The Concept of Flat-Pack Furniture 29

2.2.2 Emphasis on Scandinavian Design and Functionality 29

2.2.3 Integration of In-Store Experience and E-Commerce 30

2.2.4 Commitment to Sustainability and Social Responsibility 31

2.2.5 Lessons for Other Companies 31

2.3 Family Involvement in IKEA's Success 32

2.3.1 The Kamprad Family Legacy 33

2.3.2 Family Values in IKEA's Corporate Culture 33

2.3.3 Family Governance and Succession Planning 34

2.3.4 Long-Term Perspective and Innovation 34

2.3.5 Lessons Learned from IKEA 35

2.4 Lessons Learned from IKEA 36

2.4.1 Embrace Simplicity and Affordability 36

2.4.2 Design for Functionality and Practicality 37

2.4.3 Create an Engaging Customer Experience 37

2.4.4 Emphasize Sustainability and Social Responsibility 38

2.4.5 Foster a Strong Company Culture 38

2.4.6 Embrace Family Involvement and Long-Term Vision 39

2.4.7 Adapt to Changing Market Trends 39

2.4.8 Invest in Employee Development and Well-being 40

Toyota... 41

  3.1 The Toyota Philosophy 41

    3.1.1 The Foundation of the Toyota Philosophy 41

    3.1.2 Respect for People.............................. 41

    3.1.3 Just-in-Time Production..................... 42

    3.1.4 Total Quality Management................. 42

    3.1.5 The Role of Family in Toyota's Success.. 42

    3.1.6 Lessons for Other Companies 43

  3.2 Family Influence in Toyota's Success 44

    3.2.1 The Toyota Family Legacy.................... 44

    3.2.2 Family Values in Toyota's Business Strategy... 45

    3.2.3 Family Involvement in Toyota's Leadership.. 46

    3.2.4 Lessons Learned from Toyota's Success 46

  3.3 Toyota's Commitment to Quality 48

    3.3.1 The Toyota Production System 48

    3.3.2 Total Quality Management................. 49

    3.3.3 Continuous Training and Development. 49

    3.3.4 Supplier Collaboration........................ 50

    3.3.5 Lessons for Other Companies 50

  3.4 Applying Toyota's Principles to Other Companies... 51

    3.4.1 Embracing Continuous Improvement.... 51

    3.4.2 Building Strong Supplier Relationships. 52

3.4.3 Prioritizing Quality and Customer Satisfaction 53

3.4.4 Empowering Employees and Promoting a Culture of Respect..53

3.4.5 Implementing Lean Manufacturing and Waste Reduction 54

3.4.6 Embracing a Long-Term Perspective......54

Ferrero...56

4.1 The Ferrero Family Legacy...........................56

4.1.1 A Sweet Beginning...............................56

4.1.2 Family Values at the Core 56

4.1.3 Innovation and Product Excellence 56

4.1.4 Balancing Tradition and Modernity.........57

4.1.5 Lessons from Ferrero's Success 58

4.2 Ferrero's Product Innovation 59

4.2.1 A Legacy of Innovation................................59

4.2.2 Creating Unique Experiences 59

4.2.3 Balancing Tradition and Innovation........60

4.2.4 Lessons from Ferrero's Success 61

4.3 Balancing Tradition and Modernity.................62

4.3.1 Embracing the Legacy 63

4.3.2 Embracing Innovation................................63

4.3.3 Nurturing Entrepreneurial Spirit 64

4.3.4 Embracing Change and Continuous Learning..65

4.3.5 Building a Strong Corporate Culture.......65

4.3.6 Lessons for Other Companies....................66

4.4 Lessons from Ferrero's Success 67

4.4.1 Embrace a Strong Family Legacy.............. 67

4.4.2 Foster a Culture of Product Innovation . 68

4.4.3 Balance Tradition and Modernity 68

4.4.4 Prioritize Quality and Excellence 69

4.4.5 Cultivate Strong Family Values 69

4.4.6 Build Strong Relationships with Suppliers and Partners 69

4.4.7 Focus on Sustainability and Corporate Social Responsibility 70

4.4.8 Adapt to Changing Market Trends 70

Patagonia 72

5.1 The Patagonia Story 72

5.1.1 The Early Years and Founding Principles 72

5.1.2 Environmental Sustainability as a Core Value 73

5.1.3 Ethical Leadership and Social Responsibility 73

5.1.4 Lessons for Other Companies 74

5.2 Patagonia's Commitment to Sustainability ... 76

5.2.1 A Vision for a Sustainable Future 76

5.2.2 Environmental Stewardship in Action ... 76

5.2.3 Transparency and Accountability 77

5.2.4 Family Values Driving Sustainability 78

5.2.5 Lessons for Other Companies 78

5.3 Family Values in Patagonia's Business Practices 80

    5.3.1 A Culture of Environmental Stewardship 80

    5.3.2 Transparency and Accountability 80

    5.3.3 Work-Life Balance and Employee Well-being 81

    5.3.4 Long-Term Thinking and Sustainable Growth 81

    5.3.5 Giving Back to the Community 81

    5.3.6 Ethical Supply Chain Practices 82

    5.3.7 Authentic Brand Storytelling 82

    5.3.8 Collaboration and Partnerships 83

5.4 Applying Patagonia's Ethical Leadership to Other Companies 83

    5.4.1 Emphasizing Environmental Responsibility 84

    5.4.2 Prioritizing Ethical Supply Chains 84

    5.4.3 Fostering a Culture of Transparency and Accountability 85

    5.4.4 Investing in Employee Well-being and Development 86

    Conclusion 87

Volkswagen 88

    6.1 The Volkswagen Family Legacy 88

    6.1.1 The Origins of Volkswagen 88

    6.1.2 Family Involvement and Leadership 88

6.1.3 Overcoming Scandals and Rebuilding Trust 89

6.1.4 Family Governance and Values 89

6.1.5 Lessons in Crisis Management 90

6.1.6 Conclusion 91

6.2 Overcoming Scandals and Rebuilding Trust . 91

6.2.1 The Volkswagen Emissions Scandal 92

6.2.2 Taking Responsibility and Accountability 92

6.2.3 Implementing Structural Changes 92

6.2.4 Strengthening Governance and Compliance 93

6.2.5 Investing in Electric Vehicles and Sustainability 93

6.2.6 Rebuilding Customer Confidence 93

6.2.7 Transparency and Communication 94

6.2.8 Learning from Mistakes 94

6.2.9 Rebuilding Trust Takes Time 94

6.2.10 Lessons for Other Companies 95

6.3 Family Governance in Volkswagen 95

6.3.1 The Volkswagen Family Legacy 95

6.3.2 Family Involvement in Decision-Making 96

6.3.3 Balancing Family and Business Interests 96

6.3.4 Succession Planning and Leadership Development 96

6.3.5 Preserving Family Values 97

6.3.6 Communication and Transparency..........97

6.3.7 Long-Term Perspective 98

6.3.8 Lessons for Other Companies....................98

6.4 Lessons in Crisis Management from Volkswagen 99

6.4.1 Transparency and Accountability..........100

6.4.2 Effective Communication.........................100

6.4.3 Swift Action and Remediation.................100

6.4.4 Learning from Mistakes............................101

6.4.5 Strengthening Corporate Governance . 101

6.4.6 Rebuilding Trust and Reputation 102

6.4.7 Collaboration and Partnerships 102

Rana 104

7.1 The Rana Family Journey 104

7.1.1 From Humble Beginnings 104

7.1.2 Innovation and Expansion.......................104

7.1.3 Family Dynamics in Rana's Business.... 105

7.1.4 Key Takeaways from Rana's Growth.... 105

7.2 Innovation and Expansion in Rana's Success 107

7.2.1 A Legacy of Innovation.............................107

7.2.2 Diversification and Market Expansion 107

7.2.3 Embracing Technology and Automation 108

7.2.4 Family Values and Entrepreneurial Spirit 108

7.2.5 Sustainability and Social Responsibility 109

7.2.6 Lessons for Other Companies 109

7.3 Family Dynamics in Rana's Business............ 111

7.3.1 Shared Vision and Values 111

7.3.2 Strong Family Bonds and Trust.............. 112

7.3.3 Succession Planning and Continuity 112

7.3.4 Open Communication and Conflict Resolution... 113

7.3.5 Balancing Family and Business.............. 113

7.3.6 Embracing Innovation and Adaptability 114

7.3.7 Conclusion 115

7.4 Key Takeaways from Rana's Growth............ 115

7.4.1 Embrace Innovation and Expansion 115

7.4.2 Maintain a Strong Focus on Quality...... 116

7.4.3 Preserve Family Values and Culture 116

7.4.4 Foster Strong Family Dynamics 117

7.4.5 Build Strong Relationships with Suppliers and Partners 118

7.4.6 Adapt to Changing Consumer Preferences 118

7.4.7 Invest in Marketing and Branding 119

Benetton 120

8.1 The Benetton Family Legacy........................... 120

8.1.1 The Origins of Benetton 120

8.1.2 Benetton's Approach to Fashion and Design 120

8.1.3 Social Responsibility in Benetton's Business 121

8.1.4 Lessons in Branding from Benetton 121

8.2 Benetton's Approach to Fashion and Design 123

8.2.1 Innovative and Diverse Designs 123

8.2.2 Social Responsibility and Ethical Practices 124

8.2.3 Effective Branding Strategies 124

8.2.4 Collaboration and Partnerships 125

8.3 Social Responsibility in Benetton's Business 126

8.3.1 A Holistic Approach to Social Responsibility 126

8.3.2 Promoting Diversity and Inclusion 127

8.3.3 Ethical Supply Chain Practices 127

8.3.4 Environmental Sustainability 127

8.3.5 Collaboration and Partnerships 128

8.3.6 Transparency and Accountability 128

8.3.7 Lessons for Other Companies 129

8.4 Lessons in Branding from Benetton 130

8.4.1 Embrace Controversy and Take a Stand 131

8.4.2 Create a Strong Visual Identity 131

8.4.3 Tell Compelling Stories 131

8.4.4 Foster Diversity and Inclusion 132

8.4.5 Align Brand Values with Business Practices 132

8.4.6 Collaborate with Influencers and Partners 133

8.4.7 Stay Relevant and Evolve with the Times 133

Zanussi 135

9.1 The Zanussi Family Story 135

9.1.1 From Humble Beginnings to Industry Leader 135

9.1.2 Embracing Technological Advancements 135

9.1.3 Family Values and Long-Term Vision .. 136

9.1.4 Lessons for Other Companies 137

9.2 Zanussi's Innovation in Home Appliances . 138

9.2.1 A Legacy of Innovation 139

9.2.2 Embracing Technological Advancements 139

9.2.3 Design and User Experience 140

9.2.4 Sustainability and Energy Efficiency 140

9.2.5 Lessons for Other Companies 141

9.3 Family Values in Zanussi's Business Strategy 142

9.3.1 A Strong Sense of Purpose 143

9.3.2 Long-Term Perspective 143

9.3.3 Strong Family Governance 144

9.3.4 Employee Engagement and Development 144

9.3.5 Customer-Centric Approach 145

9.3.6 Innovation and Adaptability 145

9.4 Applying Zanussi's Adaptability to Other Industries 146

9.4.1 Embracing Change and Innovation 147

9.4.2 Customer-Centric Approach 147

9.4.3 Flexibility and Agility 148

9.4.4 Strong Leadership and Family Values . 148

9.4.5 Collaboration and Partnerships 149

Diesel 151

10.1 The Diesel Family Legacy 151

10.1.1 The Origins of Diesel 151

10.1.2 Diesel's Unique Branding and Marketing 151

10.1.3 Family Influence in Diesel's Creative Direction 152

10.1.4 Lessons in Brand Identity from Diesel 153

10.2 Diesel's Unique Branding and Marketing . 154

10.2.1 The Birth of a Brand 154

10.2.2 Embracing Creativity and Innovation 155

10.2.3 Authenticity and Storytelling 155

10.2.4 Engaging with the Consumer 156

10.2.5 Lessons for Other Companies 156

10.3 Family Influence in Diesel's Creative Direction 158

10.3.1 The Diesel Family Legacy 158

10.3.2 Diesel's Unique Branding and Marketing 158

10.3.3 Family Influence in Diesel's Creative Direction 159

10.3.4 Lessons in Brand Identity from Diesel 159

10.4 Lessons in Brand Identity from Diesel 161

10.4.1 Embrace Unconventional and Edgy Branding 161

10.4.2 Tell a Compelling Brand Story 161

10.4.3 Consistency in Brand Messaging 162

10.4.4 Engage with the Target Audience 162

10.4.5 Adapt to Changing Consumer Preferences 163

10.4.6 Authenticity and Transparency 164

10.4.7 Stay True to Your Brand DNA 164

Luxottica 166

11.1 The Luxottica Family Journey 166

11.1.1 From Humble Beginnings to Global Dominance 166

11.1.2 Vertical Integration: A Strategic Advantage 167

11.1.3 Family Values at the Core 167

11.1.4 Lessons Learned from Luxottica's Success 168

11.2 Luxottica's Vertical Integration Strategy . 169

11.2.1 The Power of Vertical Integration 170

11.2.2 Design and Manufacturing Excellence 170

11.2.3 Distribution and Retail Dominance.... 171

11.2.4 Key Takeaways from Luxottica's Success 171

11.3 Family Values in Luxottica's Business Model 173

11.3.1 A Family-Centric Approach 174

11.3.2 Long-Term Vision and Stability 174

11.3.3 Strong Corporate Governance 175

11.3.4 Employee Engagement and Development 175

11.3.5 Customer-Centric Approach 176

11.3.6 Lessons for Other Companies 176

11.4 Key Takeaways from Luxottica's Success 177

11.4.1 Embrace Vertical Integration 178

11.4.2 Focus on Branding and Licensing 178

11.4.3 Prioritize Innovation and Design 178

11.4.4 Nurture a Strong Company Culture.... 179

11.4.5 Adapt to Changing Market Conditions 179

11.4.6 Foster Strong Relationships with Suppliers and Retail Partners 180

11.4.7 Invest in Corporate Social Responsibility 180

11.4.8 Continuously Improve Customer Experience 181

Maina 182

12.1 The Maina Family Legacy 182

12.1.1 A Rich History................................ 182

12.1.2 Commitment to Traditional Baking ... 182

12.1.3 Family Involvement in Quality Control
.... 183

12.1.4 Lessons in Artisanal Excellence........... 184

12.2 Maina's Commitment to Traditional Baking
.... 185

12.2.1 Preserving Traditional Recipes and
Techniques 186

12.2.2 Sourcing the Finest Ingredients 186

12.2.3 Quality Control and Attention to Detail
.... 187

12.2.4 Innovation while Preserving Tradition
.... 187

12.2.5 Building a Strong Family Culture........ 188

12.2.6 Lessons for Other Companies............... 188

12.3 Family Involvement in Maina's Quality
Control.. 189

12.3.1 A Commitment to Excellence............... 190

12.3.2 Hands-On Approach............................. 190

12.3.3 Expertise and Knowledge 190

12.3.4 Training and Development.................... 191

12.3.5 Quality Control Systems 191

12.3.6 Attention to Detail 191

12.3.7 Customer Feedback and Continuous
Improvement.. 192

12.3.8 Maintaining Tradition and Innovation 192

12.3.9 Leading by Example 192

12.3.10 Lessons for Other Companies 193

12.4 Lessons in Artisanal Excellence from Maina 194

12.4.1 Preserving Tradition and Craftsmanship 194

12.4.2 Attention to Ingredients and Sourcing 195

12.4.3 Continuous Improvement and Innovation 195

12.4.4 Building Strong Relationships with Customers 196

12.4.5 Balancing Tradition and Adaptability 197

Kaiser 198

13.1 The Kaiser Family Story 198

13.1.1 From Humble Beginnings 198

13.1.2 Innovation in Food Production 198

13.1.3 Family Values in Kaiser's Business Strategy 199

13.1.4 Applying Kaiser's Expansion Strategies to Other Companies 200

13.2 Kaiser's Innovation in Food Production ... 201

13.2.1 A Legacy of Quality and Tradition 202

13.2.2 Embracing Innovation in Food Production 202

13.2.3 Family Values Driving Success 203

13.2.4 Applying Kaiser's Expansion Strategies to Other Companies 203

13.3 Family Values in Kaiser's Business Strategy 205

13.3.1 A Strong Sense of Unity and Purpose 205

13.3.2 Long-Term Vision and Commitment . 205

13.3.3 Trust and Empowerment 206

13.3.4 Ethical and Responsible Practices 206

13.3.5 Nurturing Relationships 207

13.3.6 Embracing Innovation 207

13.3.7 Balancing Tradition and Adaptability 207

13.3.8 Investing in Employee Development 208

13.3.9 Giving Back to the Community 208

13.3.10 Lessons for Other Companies 209

13.4 Applying Kaiser's Expansion Strategies to Other Companies 209

13.4.1 Embrace Innovation and Adaptability 210

13.4.2 Focus on Quality and Customer Satisfaction 210

13.4.3 Establish Strategic Partnerships 211

13.4.4 Invest in Branding and Marketing 211

13.4.5 Foster a Strong Company Culture 212

13.4.6 Expand Geographically 212

Esselunga 214

14.1 The Esselunga Family Legacy 214

14.1.1 The Founding of Esselunga 214

14.1.2 The Family's Commitment to Excellence 214

14.1.3 Customer-Centric Approach 215

14.1.4 Innovation and Adaptability 215

14.1.5 Family Involvement and Leadership . 215

14.1.6 Employee Engagement and Development 216

14.1.7 Community Involvement and Social Responsibility 216

14.1.8 Key Takeaways from Esselunga's Success 216

14.2 Esselunga's Customer-Centric Approach . 217

14.2.1 A Legacy of Customer Service 218

14.2.2 Creating a Unique Shopping Experience 218

14.2.3 Personalized Customer Service 218

14.2.4 Quality Products and Competitive Pricing 219

14.2.5 Innovation and Technology 219

14.2.6 Community Engagement and Social Responsibility 220

14.2.7 Continuous Improvement and Feedback 220

14.2.8 Lessons for Other Companies 220

14.3 Family Involvement in Esselunga's Retail Strategy 222

14.3.1 A Family Legacy of Retail Expertise ... 222

14.3.2 A Customer-Centric Approach 223

14.3.3 Innovation and Adaptability 223

14.3.4 Maintaining a Strong Company Culture
.... 224

14.3.5 Lessons for Other Companies 225

14.4 Key Takeaways from Esselunga's Success 226

14.4.1 Customer-Centric Approach 226

14.4.2 Emphasis on Quality 227

14.4.3 Innovation and Adaptability 227

14.4.4 Strong Family Involvement 228

14.4.5 Community Engagement and Social
Responsibility 228

14.4.6 Continuous Improvement and Learning
.... 229

Unleashing Power - A Symphony of Success 230

www.ingramcontent.com/pod-product-compliance
Lightning Source LLC
Chambersburg PA
CBHW051250250726
48656CB00004B/1221